QUICK LEARN BASICS OF COMPUTER

Quick Learn Basics of Computer

Author
Tiruveedula Gopikrishna
and
Dr. Mohamed A. Abdelhadi

KALPAZ

ISBN : 978-93-5128-074-3
Price : ₹ 495

First Published 2014

Published by

Kalpaz Publications
C-30, Satyawati Nagar,
Delhi-110052
Ph. : 9212142040
E-mail: kalpaz@hotmail.com

Laser Typesetting : Rudra Computer Graphics, Delhi
Printed at : G. Print Process, Delhi

Cataloging in Publication Data—DK
Courtesy: D.K. Agencies (P) Ltd.
<docinfo@dkagencies.com>

Gopikrishna, Tiruveedula.
Quick learn basics of computer / author, Tiruveedula Gopikrishna and Mohamed A. Abdelhadi.

p. cm.
Includes index.
ISBN 9789351280743

1. Computers. I. Abdelhadi, Mohamed A., joint author. II. Title.

DDC 004 23

Contents

Preface

We are very glad to present this book entitled, "Quick Learn Basics of Computer" which will help to understand primary concept of fundamental knowledge of computer of all beginners and students.

We are as authors of this book, pleased to inform you that this basics which is considered as easy by most of the beginners and students as well, is made simple and interesting. We have also made a considerable effort to see that each unit is self-contained and avoids unnecessary and unwarranted dependence on other units. Because of this, book also serves as a basic text book for all students and beginners.

We along with the technical team of publications took atmost care, to see that fundamentals of all the concepts are explained in simple and lucid language. We also worked hard in providing appropriate illustrations and examples. Because of these basics, this book is not only reader friendly but also fast reckoner for learning during the gaining fundamental knowledge of computer and in how computers used in real world.

For better understanding of the basics of computers step by step in the book has been divided into 8 units.

Unit-I : Basics of Computer and its History

Unit-II : Computer Hardware

Unit-III.	:	Computer Software
Unit-IV	:	Data, Data Processing, Information
Unit-V	:	Internet
Unit-VI	:	Introduction to Algorithms
Unit-VII	:	Introduction to Flowcharts
Unit-VIII	:	Operating System Concepts

Overview of the book

The Unit-I provides a broad introduction and history of the computer: basic definitions are given, importance of computers in real world, characteristics of computers, classification of computers,and basic architecture of computer discussed in detail.

In Unit-II, we deal with all types of computer hardware like input/output devices parts of CPU, storage devices.

In Unit-III, we describe different types of software's and their usage in real world.

In Unit-IV, describes about data, information and also discussed typesof electronic data processing.

In Unit-V, introduces the history of internet and use of internet and presents the main idea of www, webservers,webpages, websites and browsers.

In Unit-VI, we introduces the basic steps how to write an algorithms and how it can help to write computer programs.

In Unit-VII, introduces the basics of flowchart and their symbols how to draw for logic.

In Unit-VIII, describes about operating system, its functionality and components

Acknowledgements

At various stages in the writing of this book, a number of people have given us invaluable comments on the manuscript. Many people have contributed to this book in one way or another. In this regard we owe a debt of gratitude to all, especially and firstly, we would like to thank our Dean of our faculty Dr.Mustafa Akash, and vice and formal deans namely Mr.Md.Saleem, Mr.Zahir.

We would also like to thank our department colleagues Mr.Sabah, Mrs.Zohra for their encouragement and painstaking efforts in bringing out this book and for their constant support and guidance while writing this book.

Our special thanks to our Sirt University for their encouragement of all this kind of scientific works. And English department colleagues Dr.Saravanan, Dr.Harpreet, Dr.Sinha, and Dr.Eldo,Dr.Sivadas,Prof Balaram,Dr.Suresh, and Dr.Dasora, Mr.D.Nageswara rao,Dr.M.Vijay Kumar for their continued support and encouragement as well.

Finally, we would like to thank and express appreciation to our parents and family members for their patience and encouragement in bringing out this book.

1

Basics of Computer and History

1.1 Introduction

1.1.1 History of computer

Computers and computer applications are on almost every aspect of our daily lives. As like many ordinary objects around us, we may need clearer understanding of what they are. You may ask "What is a computer?" or "What is a software", or "What is a programming language?" First, let's examine the history.

1. The history of computers starts out about 2000 years ago in Babylonia (Mesopotamia), at the birth of the

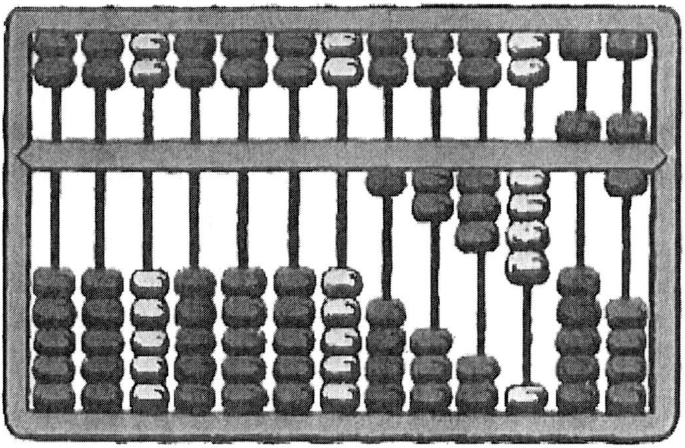

abacus, a wooden rack holding two horizontal wires with beads strung on them.

2. Blaise Pascal is usually credited for building the first *digital computer* in 1642. It added numbers entered with dials and was made to help his father, a tax collector. The basic principle of his calculator is still used today in water meters and modern-day odometers. Instead of having a carriage wheel turn the gear, he made each ten-teeth wheel accessible to be turned directly by a person's hand (later inventors added keys and a crank), with the result that when the wheels were turned in the proper sequences, a series of numbers was entered and a cumulative sum was obtained. The gear train supplied a mechanical answer equal to the answer that is obtained by using arithmetic.

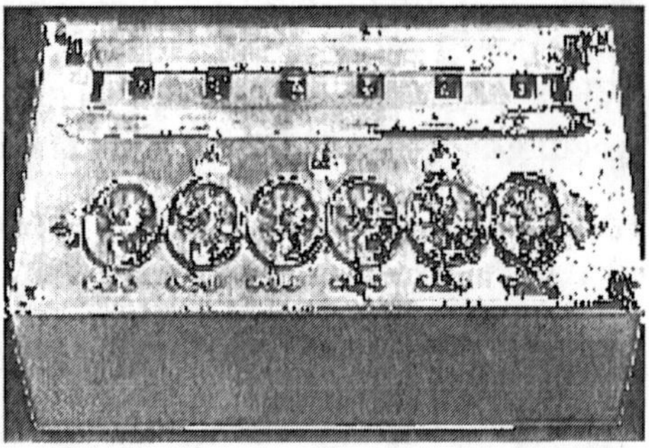

This first mechanical calculator, called the Pascaline, had several disadvantages. Although it did offer a substantial improvement over manual calculations, only Pascal himself could repair the device and it cost more than the people it replaced! In addition, the first signs of technophobia emerged with mathematicians fearing the loss of their jobs due to progress.

3. A step towards automated computing was the development of *punched cards*, which were first

successfully used with computers in 1890 by *Herman Hollerith*and James Powers, who worked for the *US. Census Bureau.* They developed devices that could read the information that had been punched into the cards automatically, without human help. Because of this, reading errors were reduced dramatically, work flow increased, and, most importantly, stacks of punched cards could be used as easily accessible memory of almost unlimited size. Furthermore, different problems could be stored on different stacks of cards and accessed when needed.

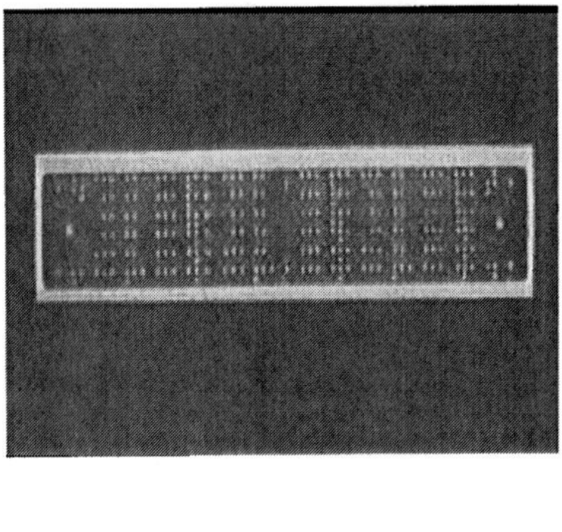

4. These advantages were seen by commercial companies and soon led to the development of improved punch-card using computers created by *International Business Machines* (IBM), Remington (yes, the same people that make shavers), Burroughs, and other corporations. These computers used electromechanical devices in which electrical power provided mechanical motion — like turning the wheels of an adding machine. Such systems included features to:
   - feed in a specified number of cards automatically
   - add, multiply, and sort
   - feed out cards with punched results
5. The start of World War II produced a large need for computer capacity, especially for the military. New weapons were made for which trajectory tables and other essential data were needed. In 1942, John P.

Eckert, *John W. Mauchly*, and their associates at the Moore school of Electrical Engineering of University of Pennsylvania decided to build a high - speed electronic computer to do the job. This machine became known as **ENIAC** (Electrical Numerical Integrator And Calculator)

Two men (in uniform) being trained to maintain the ENIAC computer. The two women in the photo were programmers. The ENIAC occupied the entire thirty by fifty feet room.

6. The size of ENIAC's numerical "word" was 10 decimal digits, and it could multiply two of these numbers at a rate of 300 per second, by finding the value of each product from a multiplication table stored in its memory. ENIAC was therefore about 1,000 times faster then the previous generation of relay computers. ENIAC used **18,000 vacuum tubes**; about 1,800 square feet of floor space, and consumed about 180,000 watts of electrical power. It had punched card I/O, 1 multiplier, 1 divider/square rooter, and 20 adders using decimal ring counters, which served as adders and also as quick-access (.0002 seconds) read-write register storage. The executable instructions making up a program were embodied in the separate "units" of ENIAC, which were plugged together to form a "route" for the flow of information.

7. Early in the 50's two important engineering discoveries changed the image of the electronic - computer field, from one of fast but unreliable hardware to an image of relatively high reliability and even more capability. These discoveries were the magnetic core memory and the Transistor –Circuit element.

   These technical discoveries quickly found their way into new models of digital computers. RAM capacities increased from 8,000 to 64,000 words in commercially available machines by the 1960's, with access times of 2 to 3 MS (Milliseconds). These machines were very expensive to purchase or even to rent and were particularly expensive to operate because of the cost of expanding programming. Such computers were mostly found in large computer centers operated by industry, government, and private laboratories - staffed with many programmers and support personnel. This situation led to modes of operation enabling the sharing of the high potential available.

Many companies, such as Apple Computer and Radio Shack, introduced very successful PC's in the 1970's, encouraged in part by a fad in computer (video) games. In the 1980's some friction occurred in the crowded PC field, with Apple and IBM keeping strong. In the manufacturing of semiconductor chips, the Intel and Motorola Corporations were very competitive into the 1980s, although Japanese firms were making strong economic advances, especially in the area of memory chips. By the late 1980s, some personal computers were run by microprocessors that, handling 32 bits of data at a time, could process about 4,000,000 instructions per second.

1.1.2. Generations of Computer

First Generation (1940-1956) Vacuum Tubes

The first computers used vacuum tubes for circuitry and *magnetic drums* for memory, and were often enormous, taking up entire rooms. They were very expensive to operate and in addition to using a great deal of electricity, generated a lot of heat, which was often the cause of malfunctions.

First generation computers relied on *machine language*, the lowest-level programming language understood by computers, to perform operations, and they could only solve one problem at a time. Input was based on punched cards and paper tape, and output was displayed on printouts.

The UNIVAC and *ENIAC*computers are examples of first-generation computing devices. The UNIVAC was the first commercial computer delivered to a business client, the U.S. Census Bureau in 1951.

Below we will see more detailed the development of this generation:

This era of modern computing began with a flurry of development before and during World War II, as *electronic circuit* elements replaced mechanical equivalents, and digital calculations replaced analog calculations. Machines such as the *Z3*, the *Atanasoff–Berry Computer, the Colossus computers,* and the *ENIAC* were built by hand using circuits containing relays or valves (vacuum tubes), and often used *punched cards* or *punched paper tape* for input and as the main (non-volatile) storage medium. This computer was defined the "first computer".

There were three parallel streams of computer development in the World War II era; the first stream largely ignored, and the second stream deliberately kept secret. The first was the German work of *Konrad Zuse.* The second was the secret development of the Colossus computers in the UK. Neither of these had much influence on the various computing projects in the United States. The third stream of computer development, Eckert and Mauchly's ENIAC and EDVAC, was widely publicized.

Alan Turing's 1936 proved enormously influential in computing and *computer science* the sequential process of the machines. Turing provided a definition of a universal computer which executes a program stored on tape. This construct came to be called a *Turing machine.* Except for the limitations imposed by their finite memory stores, modern computers are said to be *Turing-complete*, which is to say, they have *algorithm* execution capability equivalent to a universal Turing machine. (This process is related with the executed process)

This computing machine to be a practical general-purpose computer, there must be some convenient read-write mechanism, punched tape, for example. With knowledge of Alan Turing's theoretical 'universal computing machine' *John von Neumann* defined an architecture which uses the same *memory* both to store programs and data: virtually all contemporary computers use this architecture (or some variant). While it is theoretically possible to implement a full computer entirely mechanically electronics made possible the speed and later the miniaturization that characterize modern computers.

In 1939, development began at IBM's Endicott laboratories on the *Harvard the first machine developed was Mark I.* Known officially as the Automatic Sequence Controlled Calculator, the Mark I was a general purpose electro-mechanical computer built with IBM financing and with assistance from IBM personnel, under the direction of Harvard mathematician Howard Aiken. Its design was influenced by Babbage's Analytical Engine, using decimal arithmetic and storage wheels and rotary switches in addition to electromagnetic relays. It was programmable via punched paper tape, and contained several calculation units working in parallel. Later versions contained several paper tape readers and the machine could switch between readers based on a condition. The Mark I was moved to *Harvard University*and began operation in May 1944.

After the Mark I, other machines developed as:

*George Stibitz*is internationally recognized as one of the fathers of the modern digital computer. While working at Bell Labs in November 1937, Stibitz invented and built a relay-based calculator that he dubbed the "Model K" (for "kitchen table", on which he had assembled it), which was the first to calculate using *binary form.*

The Atanasoff-Berry Computer was the world's first electronic digital computer. The design used over 300 vacuum tubes and employed capacitors fixed in a mechanically rotating drum for memory. Though the ABC machine was not programmable, it was the first to use electronic tubes in an adder.

But one the machine most representative of this generation was the US-built ENIAC (Electronic Numerical Integrator and Computer) was the first electronic general-purpose computer. It combined, for the first time, the high speed of electronics with the ability to be programmed for many complex problems. It could add or subtract 5000 times a second, a thousand times faster than any other machine. High speed memory was limited to 20 words (about 80 bytes).

ENIAC's development and construction lasted from 1943 to full operation at the end of 1945. The machine was huge, weighing 30 tons, and contained over 18,000 vacuum tubes. One of the major engineering feats was to minimize tube burnout, which was a common problem at that time. The machine was in almost constant use for the next ten years.

Even before the ENIAC was finished, Eckert and Mauchly recognized its limitations and started the design of a stored-program computer, EDVAC (Electronic Discrete Variable Automatic Computer). *John von Neumann* was credited with a *widely circulated report*describing the *EDVAC* design in which both the programs and working data were stored in a single, unified store. This basic design, denoted the *von Neumann architecture*, would serve as the foundation for the worldwide development of ENIAC's successors. In this generation of equipment, temporary or working storage was provided by *acoustic delay lines*, which used the propagation time of sound through a medium such as liquid *mercury* (or through a wire) to briefly store data. A series of *acoustic* pulses is sent along a tube; after a time, as the pulse reached the end of the tube, the circuitry detected whether the pulse represented a 1 or 0 and caused the oscillator to re-send the pulse. Others used *Williams's tubes*, which use the ability of a small cathode-ray tube (CRT) to store and retrieve data as charged areas on the phosphor screen. By 1954, *magnetic core memory*was rapidly displacing most other forms of temporary storage, and dominated the field through the mid-1970s.

EDVAC was the first stored-program computer designed; however it was not the first to run. In 1949 by the *Manchester Mark 1*computer, a complete system, using Williams's tube and *magnetic drum* memory, and introducing *index registers*.

With EDVAC the first generation of computers ends and then starts the second generation using transistors.

Second Generation (1956-1963) Transistors

From 1955 the transistors replaced *vacuum tubes* in computer designs, giving rise to the "second generation" of computers.

*Transistors*replaced vacuum tubes and ushered in the second generation of computers. The transistor was invented in 1947 but did not see widespread use in computers until the late 1950s. Also the first computers of this generation were developed for the atomic energy industry.

The Second-generation of computers moved from cryptic*binary*machine language to symbolic, or *assembly*, languages, which allowed programmers to specify instructions in words. *High-level programming languages* were also being developed at this time, such as early versions of *COBOL* and *FORTRAN*. These were also the first computers that stored their instructions in their memory, which moved from a magnetic drum to magnetic core *technology*.

The transistor was far superior to the vacuum tube, allowing computers to become smaller, faster, cheaper, more energy-efficient and more reliable than their first-generation predecessors. Though the transistor still generated a great deal of heat that subjected the computer to damage, it was a vast improvement over the vacuum tube. Second-generation computers still relied on punched cards for input and printouts for output.

The first *transistorised computer* was built at the *University of Manchester* and was operational by 1953; a second version was completed there in April 1955. The later machine used 200 transistors and 1,300 *solid-statediodes* and had a power consumption of 150 watts. However, it still required valves to generate the clock waveforms at 125 kHz and to read and write on the magnetic *drum memory.*

Compared to vacuum tubes, transistors have many advantages: they are smaller, and require less power than vacuum tubes, so give off less heat. Silicon junction transistors were much more reliable than vacuum tubes and had longer, indefinite, service life. Transistorized computers could contain tens of thousands of binary logic circuits in a relatively compact space. Transistors greatly reduced computers' size, initial cost, and *operating cost.*

Transistorized electronics improved not only the *CPU* (Central Processing Unit), but also the *peripheral devices.* The *IBM 350*RAMAC was introduced in 1956 and was the world's first disk drive. The second generation *disk data storage units.*

A removable disk stack can be easily exchanged with another stack in a few seconds. Even if the removable disks' capacity is smaller than fixed disks,' their inter-changeability guarantees a nearly unlimited quantity of data close at hand. *Magnetic tape* provided archival capability for this data, at a lower cost than disk.

Many second generation CPUs delegated peripheral device communications to a secondary processor. For example, while the communication processor controlled *card reading and punching,* the main CPU executed calculations and binary *branch instructions.*

During the second generation *remote terminal* units like telephone connections provided sufficient speed for early remote terminals and allowed hundreds of kilometres separation between remote-terminals and the computing center. Eventually these stand-alone computer networks would be generalized into an interconnected network of networks—the internet. These developments were the precedent for what we now know as internet

Third Generation (1964-1971) ***Integrated Circuits***

The development of the *integrated circuit* was the hallmark of the third generation of computers. Transistors were miniaturized and placed on *siliconchips,* called *semiconductors,* which drastically increased the speed and efficiency of computers.

The explosion in the use of computers began with "third-generation" computers, making use of *JackSt. Clair Kilby*'s and *Robert Noyce*'s independent invention of the integrated circuit (or microchip), which later led to the invention of the microprocessor, by *Ted Hoff, Federico Faggin,* and Stanley Mazor at *Intel.*

Instead of punched cards and printouts, users interacted with third generation computers through *keyboards* and *monitors* and *interfaced* with an *operating system,* which allowed the device to run many different *applications* at one time with a central program that monitored the memory. Computers for the first time became accessible to a mass audience because they were smaller and cheaper than their predecessors.

The *computer* became small, low-cost and that could be owned by individuals and small businesses.

Microcomputers, the first of which appeared in the 1970s, became ubiquitous in the 1980s and beyond. *Steve Wozniak*, co-founder of *Apple Computer*, is sometimes erroneously credited with developing the first mass-market *home computers*.

Fourth Generation (1971-80's) Microprocessors

The *microprocessor* brought the fourth generation of computers, as thousands of *integrated circuits* were built onto a single silicon chip. What in the first generation filled an entire room could now fit in the palm of the hand. The *Intel* 4004 chip, developed in 1971, located all the components of the computer—from the *central processing unit* and memory to input/output controls—on a single chip.

In 1981 *IBM* introduced its first computer for the home user, and in 1984 *Apple* introduced the Macintosh. Microprocessors also moved out of the realm of desktop computers and into many areas of life as more and more everyday products began to use microprocessors.

As these small computers became more powerful, they could be linked together to form networks, which eventually led to the development of the *Internet*. Fourth generation computers also saw the development of, the *mouse* and *handheld* devices, etc.

Fifth Generation (Present and Beyond) Artificial Intelligence

Fifth generation computing devices, based on *artificial intelligence*, are still in development, though there are some *applications*, such as *voice recognition*, that are being used today. The use of *parallel processing* and superconductors is helping to make artificial intelligence a reality. *Quantum computation* and molecular and *nanotechnology* will radically change the face of computers in years to come. The goal of fifth-generation computing is to develop devices that respond to *natural language* input and are capable of learning and self-organization.

1.2 What is Computer?

Computer is an electronic machine that takes data and instructions, processes data according to the given instructions, gives results and stores them for later use.

Today, computers are being used in every field of life. It can be used for different tasks. It is used for data processing. It is used to calculate or perform some mathematical work. It can be used for word processing, record keeping, listening music, playing computer games etc. And above all, it is being used to access Internet.

1.2.1 What are Characteristics of Computer?

Following are the important characteristics of a computer:

1. Speed

   Computers work at a very high speed. They are much faster than humans.

A computer can perform billions of calculations in a second. Computer speed is measured in Mega Hertz (MHz).

2. Storage
   Computer can store large amounts of data permanently.

3. Processing
   A computer can process the given instructions. It can perform different types of processing like addition, subtraction, multiplication and division.

4. Accuracy
   Accuracy means the capability to provide results without any errors. Computer can process large amounts of data and produce 100% accurate results.

5. Recalling
   A computer can recall the stored data and information at any time, as and when required.

6. CostReduction
   Computer can reduce cost. We can do a work in less time and cost by computer. A single person, with computer, can do work of many people in an office.

8. Versatile
   A computer can perform different types of tasks. We can use a computer in hospital, bank or at home.

9. No Feelings
   Computer has no feelings. It cannot be affected by sorrows and happiness.

10. No Intelligence
    Computer itself is not intelligent. It only follows the given instructions. If a computer is given a program for addition it cannot perform subtraction by itself.

    You might also like:

1.2.2 What are the basic units or components of a computer?

Following are the main basic components of the computer:

1. Input Unit
2. Output Unit
3. Central Processing Unit (CPU / Processor)
4. Memory Unit
5. Storage Unit

1. Input Unit

Input unit consists of *input devices.* Input devices are used to enter data and instructions into computer memory. Examples of input devices are Keyboard, mouse, joystick and microphone etc.

2. Output Unit

Output unit consists of *output devices.* Output devices are used to show results produced by computer after data processing. Examples of output devices are Monitor, Printer, plotter and speaker etc.

3. Central Processing Unit

Central processing unit is also called *CPU or Processor.* It is the brain of the computer. It performs data processing. It controls overall operations and components of the computer.

4. Memory Unit

Memory unit consists of memory devices to store data. For Example *RAM* is most common example of memory.

5. Storage Unit

Storage unit consists of s*torage media.* Storage media are used to store large amounts of data permanently. Examples of storage media are Hard disk, CD, DVD and Zip disk etc.

1.3 What are Different Types of Computer?

Computers can be divided into the following 3 types on the basis of their working mechanism:

(1) Analog Computers

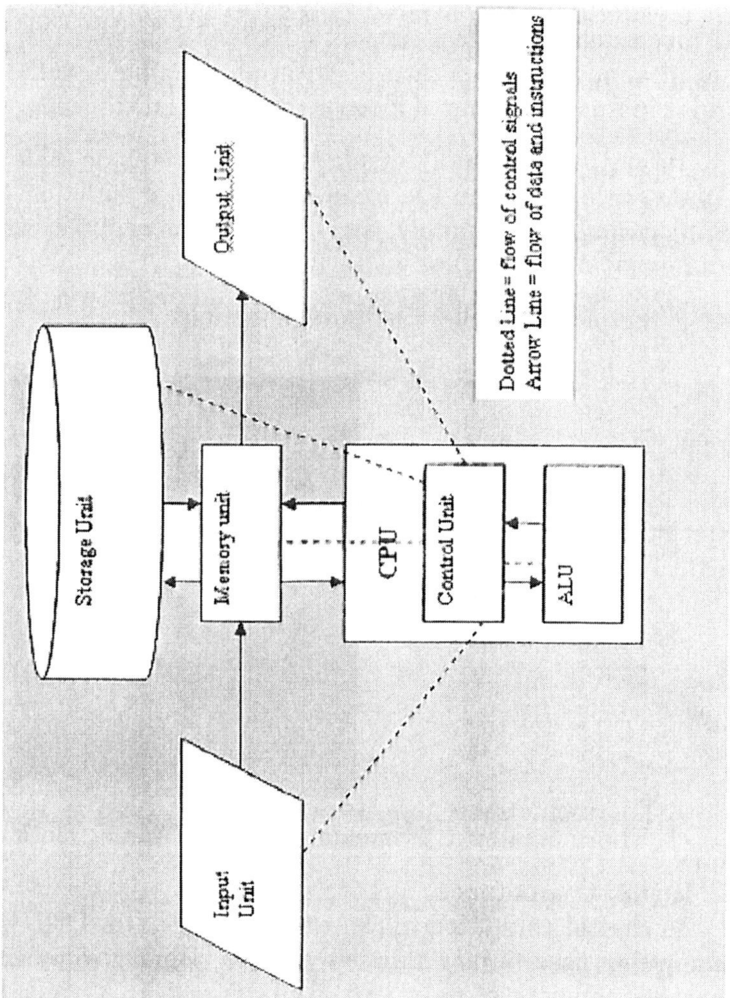
Storage Unit
Memory unit
CPU
Control Unit
ALU
Input Unit
Output Unit
Dotted Line = flow of control signals
Arrow Line = flow of data and instructions

(2) Digital Computers

(3) Hybrid Computers

1. Analog Computers

Analog computer is used to measure continuous values. It measures a physical property like voltage, pressure, speed, time and temperature. An analog computer takes input in analog form and gives output in analog form.

Its output is usually displayed on a meter or scale. Analog computer has low memory and fewer functions. Analog computer is mainly used in the field of engineering and medicine. Examples include:

Examples of Analog Computers include:

1. Thermometer 2.Speedometer 3. Analog clock

2. Digital Computers

A digital computer works with digital data. Digital computer uses binary number system. Binary number system consists of only two digits 0 and 1. A digital computer represents data in digital dignals. A 0 represents OFF and a 1 represents ON. Digital computer performs arithmetic and logical operations on data. It gives output in digital form.

Digital computers are very fast. These computers can store results. They have large Memory (that is data storing capacity). Today most of the computers used in offices and homes are Digital computers.

Examples:

1. Personal Computer-(also called PC or Micro Computer)
2. Digital Score board
3. Digital watch

3. Hybrid Computers

A hybrid computer is a combination of both analog and digital computer. Hybrid computer can handle both analog and digital data. A hybrid computer combines the best characteristics of both the analog and digital computer. It can accept data in both analog and digital form.

Examples:

1. Hybrid computer devices are used in hospitals that may calculate patient's heart function, temperature and blood pressure etc. This calculation may be converted into numbers and shown in digital form. For example,

The Vital Signs Monitoring unit

also called VSM in short. It has Blood Pressure monitor, ECG monitor, respiratory monitor, and is also used for monitoring anesthesia.

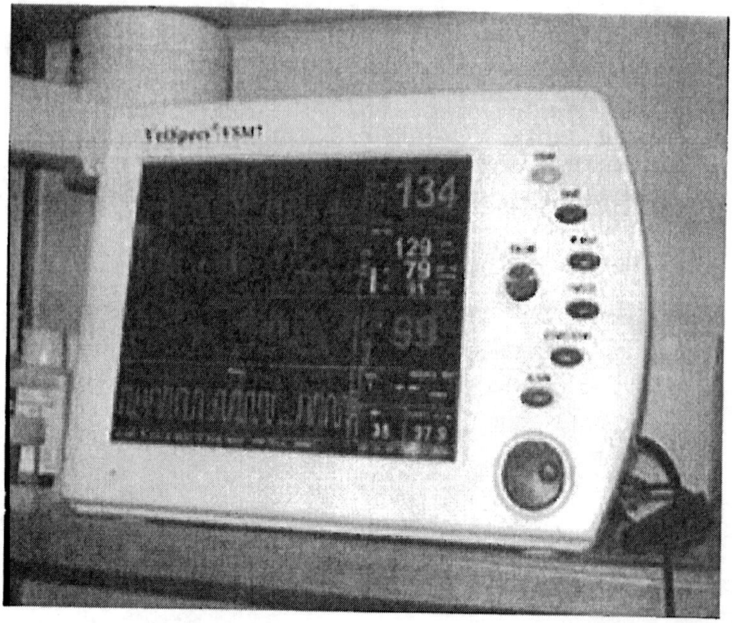

2. Hybrid computers are also used in spaceships and missile system.
3. Hybrid Computer Machines are generally used in scientific applications
4. Hybrid computers are used for controlling industrial processes.

Write a note on Classification of Computers

1.3.1 Write a note on "Classification of Computers" OR Explain Types of computer on the basis of Size, Shape and Resources.

Classification of Computers

Computers are classified on the basis of size, speed and price as under:

- Microcomputer or Personal Computer
- Mini Computer

- Mainframe Computer
- Super Computer

1. Micro Computers

Desktop Model computer

Micro computer is also called personal computer. It was introduced in 1970. It contains input devices, output device, storage device, memory and processor. It is used by one person at a time. Examples of personal computers are PC and Apple Macintosh. The major types of personal computers are desktop computer and portable computer.

Desktop Computers

Tower Model computer

These computers can easily fit on a table or desktop, hence the name. These computers come in two models or casings. In Desktop model, the system unit is placed on the desktop or table. Monitor is placed on the system unit. In Tower model, both monitor and system unit are placed on the table.

Portable Computer

Portable is a personal computer that can be carried from one place to other easily. Notebook computer and

Lap top computer or notebook computer

Hand held computer

handheld computer (smart phone) are examples of portable computers. Notebook computer is also called laptop computer. Laptop computers are very small in size and can be placed easily on lap.

Handheld Computers (like smart phone) are also potable. Handheld computer is also known as palmtop computer. It easily fits in the hand of the user.

Uses of Micro Computer

The PC is the most common type of computer used in the office. It is now widely used in many homes. These are also used for business and engineering application.

2. Mini Computers

Mini computers were introduced in the 1960s. Minicomputer is larger and more powerful computer than personal computer. It can execute five million instructions per second. It generally consists of two or more processors.

Mini computer can serve up to 4000 connected users simultaneously. It is normally accessed by users via personal computer or terminal. A device with a monitor and keyboard is called terminal. It is also known as dumb terminal. It has no processing power and cannot work as stand-alone computer. Examples of mini computers are:

- AX-8800
- AS400.

Uses of Mini Computers

Mini computers are often used by small and medium-sized companies to provide centralized store of information.

3.Mainframe Computers

Mainframe computers were introduced in 1975. A mainframe computer is a very large computer in size. It is more powerful than mini computer. It consists of multiple processors. It is designed to perform multiple tasks for multiple users at the same time. Mainframe computers can serve up to 50,000 users at the same time.

The users access a mainframe computer through terminal or personal computer. A typical mainframe computer can execute 16 million instructions per second. Examples of mainframe computers are

- NEC 610
- DEC 10

Uses of Mainframe Computers

Mainframe computers are used in large organizations. For example, airlines use these computers for ticket reservation system. NADRA - The Computerized National Identity Card Issuer in Pakistan – uses mainframe computers to maintain the information of population.

4. Super Computers

Super computers were introduced in 1980s. Super computer is the fastest computer. Super computer is the biggest in size and the most expensive in price than any other computers.

It is the most sophisticated, complex and advanced computer. It has a very large storage capacity. It can process trillions of instructions in one second. Super Computer is the fastest and most powerful computer of a time. Supercomputers are veryexpensive. Supercomputers are used for highly calculation-intensive tasks. Super computers are used for specialized applications that require immense amounts of mathematical calculations. Supercomputers were designed primarily by computer scientist - Seymour Cray at Control Data Corporation (CDC).

Uses of Super Computers include:

1. Weather forecasting,
2. Animated graphics like in Hollywood movies,
3. Fluid dynamic calculations,
4. Nuclear energy research,
5. Space science
6. Weapon and missile design
7. and petroleum exploration etc.

Today, supercomputers are produced by traditional companies such as Cray, IBM and Hewlett- Packard, who had purchased many of the 1980s companies to gain their experience. Since October 2010, the Tianhe-1A supercomputer has been the fastest in the world; it is located in China. The main difference between a supercomputer and a mainframe is that a supercomputer channels all its power into executing a single program as fast as possible, whereas a mainframe uses its power to execute many programs concurrently. The modern super computer consists of thousands of microprocessors. Super computer uses high-speed facilities such as satellite for online processing. Examples of super computers are CRAY-XP, ETA-10, and Deep Blue and above all Todays number one super computer is Tianhe-1A supercomputer of China. Aircraft companies use super computer to simulate aircraft and check its performance. Many Hollywood movies use it for animation purposes.

1.4 What are the basic operations of a computer?

There are five basic operations of a computer as follows:

1. Inputting

It is the process of entering data and instructions into computer system. Input is performed by input devices like keyboard, mouse, scanner, digital camera and microphone etc.

2. Storing

It is the process of saving data and instructions to make them available as and when required in future. Data and programs are stored on permanent storage devices, especially on hard disk. Other permanent storage media include CD - Compact Disk, DVD - Digital Video Disk and Zip Disk etc.

3. Processing

It is the process of performing arithmetic and logical operations on data to convert them into useful information. Processing is performed by CPU- Central Processing Unit. CPU is also called Processor. It is the brain of computer.

4. Outputting

It is the process of producing useful information after processing data, for example, printed reports for user. Output is presented by output devices like monitor, printer and speakers.

5. Controlling

It is the process of directing and controlling the manner and sequence in which all above operations are performed. Control Unit will control operations and components of a computer. Control Unit is a part of the processor.

1.5 Explain the Concept of a Computer System

A system is a set of inter related components that work together to fulfill a purpose. For example a Road Transportation System will consist of the parts - roads, vehicles- trucks, buses, vans, cars etc, passengers, the staff for ticketing and maintenance of vehicles and roads etc. And the transportation system will fulfill the purpose of carrying of passengers and luggage from place to place. Computer system consists of the following four parts:

1. Hardware
2. Software
3. Data
4. User

1. Hardware

The mechanical devices that makeup the computer are called HARDWARE, for example, Keyboard, hard disk,

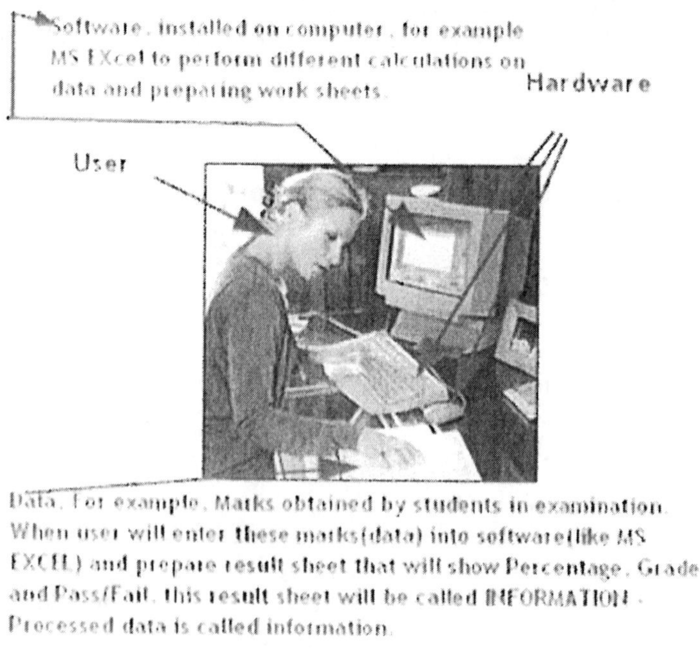

monitor, processor and mother board etc. Hardware are physical devices. They can be touched. Hardware device are interconnected and perform input, processing and output operations.

2. Software

Software is the set of instructions given to computer to perform a task. Software tells the computer what to do. System Software like operating systems are used to manage components and operations of computer. Application Software like MS Word and MS Excel are used to solve specific problems of the user, for example creating documents or preparing Student Result Sheet etc. Thousands of different software are available for use on PC.

3. Data

Data is the collection of raw facts. Data processing is the primary job of a computer. Computer processes data in many ways to convert them into useful information. Processed data becomes information. For example, during census, data of all citizens is collected. Census data is used to get report/information about total population of a country and literacy rate etc.

4. Users

People that operate the computer are called computer operators or computer users. Users use computer to solve different problems. For example, in a college a computer operator in Examination Section will feed marks obtained by students in software like MS Excel. He/ She will perform certain functions and formulae to calculate percentage and grade of each student and prepare a result sheet. This result sheet will show the marks obtained, percentage, grade and Fail/ Pass status of every student.

1.6 What are uses of computer at Home

Uses of Computer

Today, computer is used in almost every field of life. The use of computer has made different tasks very easy for us. Computer has made a very vital impact on our society. People are using computers for performing different tasks quickly and easily. In fact, computer has made our life more comfortable.

Uses of Computer at Home

Computer can be used at home in the following ways:

1. Home Budget

2. Computer can be used to manage the home budget. You can easily calculate your expenses and income with the help of software like Microsoft Excel. In MS Excel you can prepare a simple worksheet to calculate your daily expenses and income.

Date	*Category*	*Amount*
January	Home	220.35
January	Food	34.00
February	Travel	65.00
February	Food	12.00
January	Food	51.00
February	Home	358.00
January	Home	15.00

2. Computer Games

   An important use of computer at home is playing games. Different types of games are available. And if you have internet connection, then you can play games online, too. You can download PC games free from many websites. Computer games are especially played by school going children.

3. Entertainment

   You can watch movies, hear songs and find information on Internet. Video and audio songs, movies, TV shows or dramas are some of the entertainment media that can be accessed by internet enabled computer.

4. Information
   You can find any type of information from Internet. You can download books to improve your knowledge. You can use search engine, specially the giant Google Search Engine, to find information you want. Internet is a huge database of knowledge on every topic.

5. E-Mail
   You can send and receive messages and information by E-Mail. You can

6. Chatting / Instant Messaging
   You can chat with your friends on Internet by instant messaging. You can also talk with them.

7. Searching For Jobs
   You can search jobs sitting at home and browsing internet on your computer. There are many job searching websites. Most of these websites provide daily Email in your inbox with the jobs postings of your interest.

8. Online Shopping

9. With the help of your computer and internet, you can buy anything online and pay by credit cards.

10. Online Banking

11. E-Banking or online banking is the great facility for maintaining your financial transactions online. Moreover, you can pay your utility bills from your account while sitting at home.

1.7 Uses of Computer in Business Organizations

Now-a-days, computers are the essential part of any business organization. Computers are used in business companies for performing different tasks like Record Maintaining, Stock management, Pay Roll Systems, Business Correspondence and Business Communication etc., Computer can be used in business in the following ways:

- Marketing
  Any business organization can use computers for marketing their products.

- Stock Exchange
  Many stock exchanges are using computers for conducting bids. Stock brokers are using computers to perform all business functions in stock exchange.

- Banks
  These days, banks are incomplete without computers. Banks are using computers to record Daily Customer Transactions. Every bank is using a customized software like Accounts Maintenance System. Accounts Maintenance System manages all customer financial dealing records through bank. The use of computers in banks has provided many benefits. It saves a lot of time and provides convenience for the customer.

- Email
  E-Mail stands for Electronic Mail. By E-Mail, you can send and receive messages. You can also attach files of different types with email message. No doubt, E-Mail is a faster and cheaper way of communication.

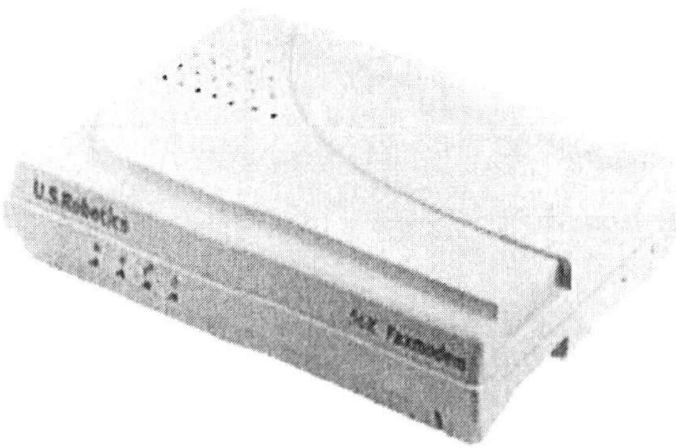

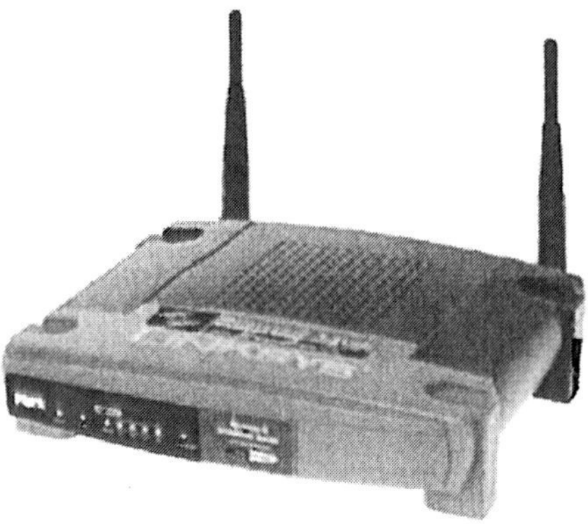

- Payroll system
  Computerized pay roll system is used in different organizations to maintain pay accounts of employees, easily and quickly.

- Stock system
  Computerized stock system is used to record number of items in stock of any organization efficiently.

- Fax
  Computers can be used to send and receive faxes. Different Fax Software are available in market for this purpose.

- 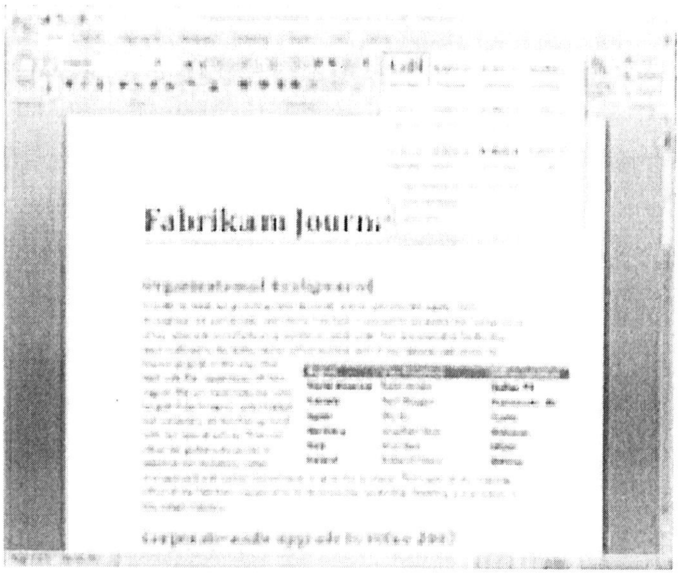

- Documentation
  Word processor software like MS Word is used to prepare different types of documents like letters, applications and other documents.

- Graphics
  Graphics software like Adobe Photoshop or Corel Draw are used for image editing and preparing posters and cards etc.

- Presentation
  Power point can be used to prepare good looking computerized presentations for business.

- Spreadsheet
  Spreadsheet software like Excel can be used to prepare computerized worksheets and carts.

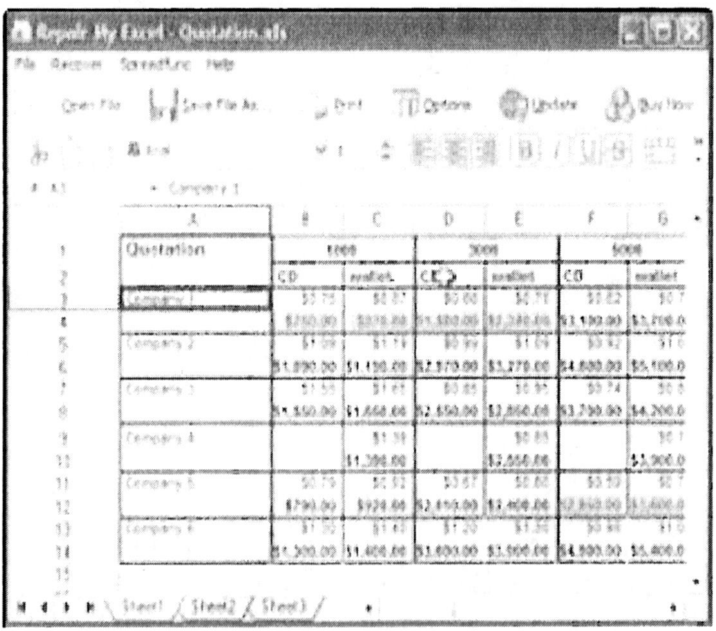

- Accounts department
  Accounts department can use Accounting software like LedgerSMB, BizCorei and Microsoft Excel to prepare

different accounting documents like balance sheet, Trial balance, Ledger and bank reconciliation etc.

1.8 Uses of Computer In Education Field

Computer can be used in education in the following ways:

- Computers In Teaching and Learning Process (Computer Aided Learning - CAL)

Computers are being used actively in educational institutes to improve the learning process. Teachers can use audio video aids through computer to prepare lesson plans. They can use Microsoft Power Point to prepare electronic presentations about their lectures. These electronic presentations will be displayed on multimedia projectors in class rooms. This will be interesting and easy to learn for students. Multimedia presentations are easy to deliver for teachers too. Computers will be helpful for:

1. Instructing the students using PowerPoint s Word documents or Web pages and using hype for better concept clarity.

2. Helps in improving pronunciation of students b microphones, headphones, speakers, specially pr software and special dedicated websites.

3. Encouraging the students to use internet, surf web pages and gather relevant detailed information through search engines.

- CBT (Computer-Based Training)
  CBT stands for Computer Based Training. In CBT, we prepare different educational programs with the help of professional teachers and audio visual aids. These educational programs are generally in the shape of lectures on a specific subject. These programs are provided on CDs.

- Online Education
  Many web sites provide online education. You can read or download educational material and books. For example, Virtual University of Pakistan is an Online Educational Institution. Students use internet to access VU website. The students log in to their accounts and e-mail boxes. They interact with different teachers online. They receive and submit their assignments and work through internet to their teachers.

- Research
  Computers are also used for research work. Internet is a huge source of information on any topic. Different researchers can share their research work using Internet.

- Institute Administration
  Computers are being used to perform many tasks in educational institutions, easily and quickly:
  - Keeping Records of students
  - Storing Records of employees of school / college
  - Managing Accounts of the institution
  - Fees collection and maintenance of fees record.
  - Circulation of instruction/notices and getting it in printed form
  - Preparation of school/ college magazine, etc.

1.9 Uses of Computer in Medical Field

Today Computers are an essential part of an hospital. Doctors and administration staff uses computers to manage patient history and medicine stocks etc. Computers play a key role in the medical field. Their uses include storing patient related data, housing knowledge bases, providing the logic and circuitry for medical equipment, scanning and imaging the body, and facilitating speedy communications. Computers can be used in medical field in the following ways:

- Hospital Administration
  We can computerize the accounting, payroll and stock system of the hospital. We can keep the record of different medicines.

- Recording Medical History Of Patients
  Computer can be used to store the medical history of the patients. Medical history is very important for patients as well as doctors. Doctors may better prescribe the medicines on the basis of the medicines used in past for a particular patient and the results obtained. Database Management System software is used to store Patient records efficiently. are stored on computer databases in the medical field. The medical history of a patient includes physical symptoms, diagnoses, treatments, and even family medical history. Details of the medications prescribed are stored together with details of any that cannot be prescribed, such as an allergy to penicillin.

  Appointments are scheduled using a computer database. Billing information is also stored. Hospitals and surgeries depend on computers for administrative and financial functions.

- Monitoring Systems
  Many computerized devices are used to monitor the blood pressure, heartbeat and brain of the patients. Computers guide in some surgical operations, too. For example in laparoscopic surgery, the surgeon inserts

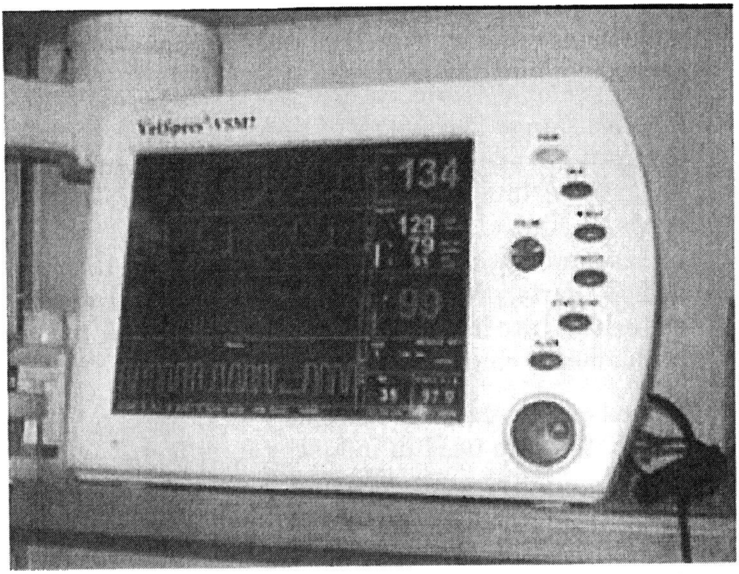

the medical tools and a small camera, and conducts the operation with the help of computers and monitors. Computers also monitor heart rates, pulse rates and brain readings. Therefore, we conclude that computers make this possible to deal with such complicated operations. It would be virtually impossible for a human to do this.

- Diagnosis of Diseases
  Computers are being used to diagnose diseases with the help of software. There are some Medical Software to diagnose diseases and prescribe medicine on the basis of symptoms.

- Life Support system
  Life support systems are used to help disabled persons, for example hearing aid device for deaf people. Latest life support devices use computer technology to help the disable people, to overcome their disabilities.

- Faster and Cheaper Communications
  Doctors and other staff can use internet to communicate to doctors in other parts of the world,

for sharing information on medical topics or even about a particular patient case. They can exchange pictures, reports and other documents, too.

- Clinical Image Processing
  Computers are being used in Medical Radiology / Diagnostic Imaging. Computers play an role in all types of clinical image processing like CT scan and ultrasound. Ultrasound uses sound waves that bounce off body parts, producing echoes. A computer translates the echoes into images, showing broken bones, muscle problems, or changes in organs, accurately.

1.10 Uses of Computer in Industry

Computers are used in industry in different types of systems. Computer-controlled robots are used to perform many complicated jobs in industry. Robots are computer controlled programmable machines. They can perform mechanical jobs, too, like pick and place different parts, welding or painting cars etc.

- Automated Production Systems
  Today, computer-controlled robots are used to assemble cars. No doubt, these systems work faster than human

beings. Another popular and efficient use for computer controlled robots is in the field of spray painting. The consistency and repeatability of a robot's motion have enabled near perfect quality painting while at the same time wasting no paint and leaving no place without paint.

Perhaps the most popular applications of robots are in industrial welding. The repeatability, uniformity quality, and speed of robotic welding is unmatched. Computer controlled Robots can be found in the manufacturing industry, the military, space exploration, transportation, and medical applications.

- Design Systems
  Computer programs are used to design the model of a product on the computer. This process is called Computer Aided Design or CAD. Due to CAD, we can test the designed product with the help of computer. When the design is completed successfully, the actual product is manufactured.

1.11 Uses of Computer in Science

Today, computers are being used in every field of life. Here we discuss Uses of Computers in Science:

Data Collection

Scientists use computers to collect data and make hypotheses on the basis of collected data.

Analysis and Testing Of Data

Scientists use computers to analyze collected data and test their hypotheses.

Exchanging Information

Scientists use computers to exchange information with their colleagues. Different Researches all over the world can share their research with one another. This will be helpful for research because this will increase the rate of completion of research projects.

Simulation of Different Events

Scientists may use computers for simulation of complex events. For example, they can use computer simulation to predict about the effects of earthquake on buildings in a particular area. They may use computer simulation to know the effects of rapid population increase on weather conditions. In fact, computer simulation of such complex events will save time as well as cost. Computer simulation can also provide a feasible solution to many problems.

Use of Computer in Medical Science

Computers may also be used to simulate the functions of parts of human body. For example, computers may simulate cell division, internal structure of molecules, a virus or bacteria attack etc.

Uses of Computer in Space Science

Computers are playing an important role to explore the outer space. The computers are mostly used to collect space data, perform experiments and prepare results. Computers are used to operate certain machines and robots to collect information from space and send it back on earth.

1.12 Differentiate between Analog and Digital Computers

The differences between analog and digital computers are as follows:

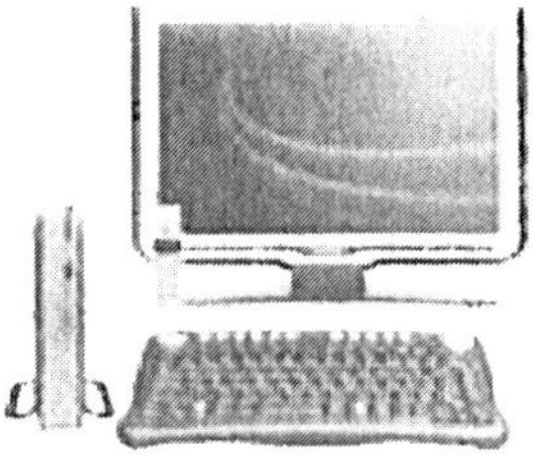

	Analog Computers	*Digital Computers*
1.	Analog Computers Work on continuous values.	Digital computers Work on discrete values.
2.	Analog Computers have low memory.	Digital computers have a very large memory
3.	Analog computers have Slow speed.	Digital computers have fast speed.
4.	Analog computers are less reliable.	Digital computers are more reliable.
5.	Analog computers used in engineering and science and medical fields.	Digital computers are used in all fields of life.
6.	Analog computers are used to calculate / measure analog quantities like speed and temperature.	Digital computers are used to calculate mathematical and logical operations. It can solve addition, subtraction, division, multiplication and other mathematical and statistical operations.
7.	Analog computers provide less accurate results.	Digital computers provide 100% accurate results.
8.	Normally Analog Computers are specific purpose	Digital Computers are general purpose
9.	Analog computers are difficult to use	Digital computers are easy to use
10.	Examples of Analog computers are: thermometer, analog clock, speedometer etc.	Examples of digital computers are: Personal Computer, laptops, smart phones etc.

2

Computer Hardware

1.1 What are Different Types of Hardware?

What is Hardware?

The physical parts of a computer are called hardware. Hardware can be touched or seen by us. For example, hard disk, mouse, keyboard, CD, CD-ROM Drive, Floppy Disk, Speakers, Modem and Printers - all are computer hardware. Different types of hardware components are as follows:

1. Input devices

Input devices are used to enter data and instructions into computer. Examples of input devices are: Keyboard, mouse, scanner, digital camera etc.

Microphone

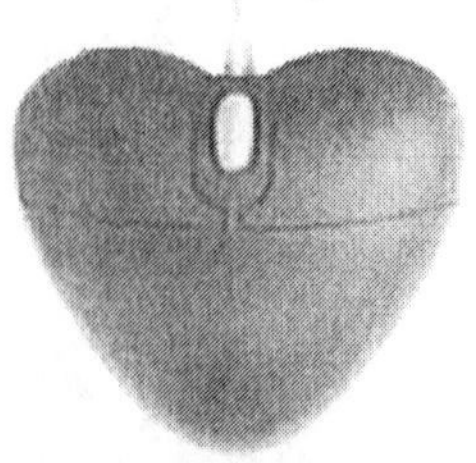

Mouse

Keyboard

2. The Central Processing unit

Central processing unit is the brain of the computer. It is also called CPU or Processor. Intel is the leading manufacturer of microprocessors. For example, Intel Pentium IV 3.2 MHz is an example of a cpu.

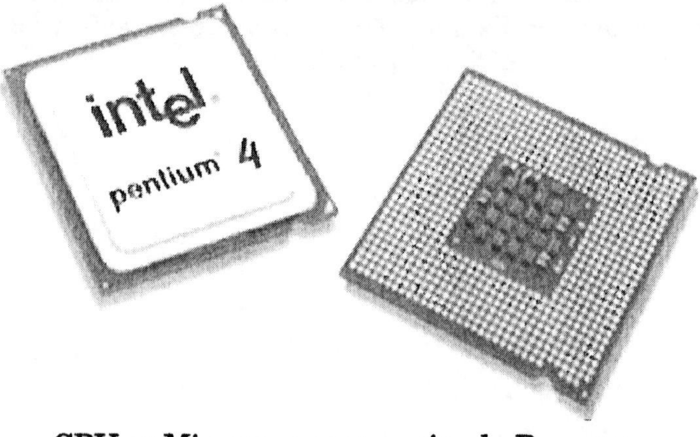

CPU or Microprocessor or simply Processor

3. Output devices

Output devices are used to show the results of processing to the user. For example monitor, printer, plotter, speaker and data projector are output devices.

Speakers

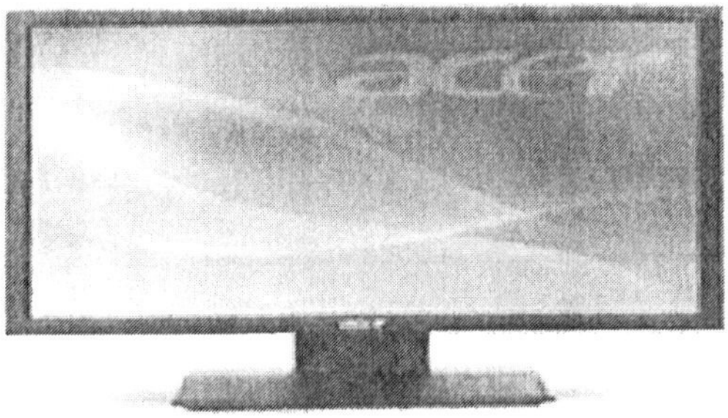

LCD Monitor

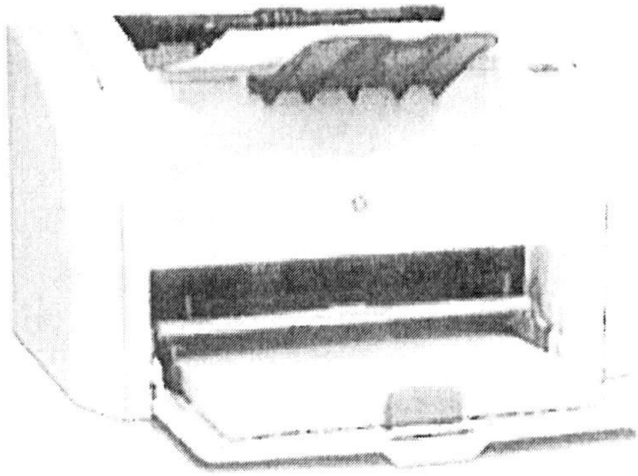

Printer

4. Memory chips

Memory is a component of a computer to store data and instructions. RAM is an example of memory chip. It stands for Random Access Memory. Every program to be executed is loaded in RAM from hard disk. CPU executes the programs loaded in RAM.RAM is a temporary memory, all data and programs are lost from RAM, when computer is turned off. ROM stands for Read Only Memory. ROM is permanent memory chip; we cannot change or delete its contents. It is a non-volatile memory.

ROM shape 1

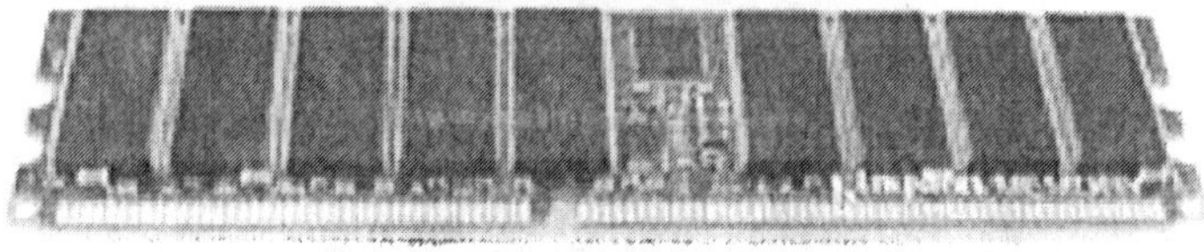

RAM

ROM shape 2

5. Storage devices

Storage Devices are used to store large amounts of data permanently. For example: hard disk, CD, DVD etc. are storage devices. Moreover, Zip Disk and Floppy disk is also considered as storage devices.

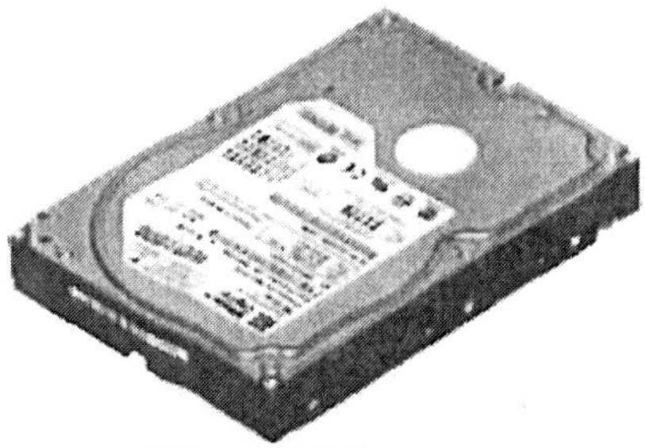

Hard Disk

DVD ROM

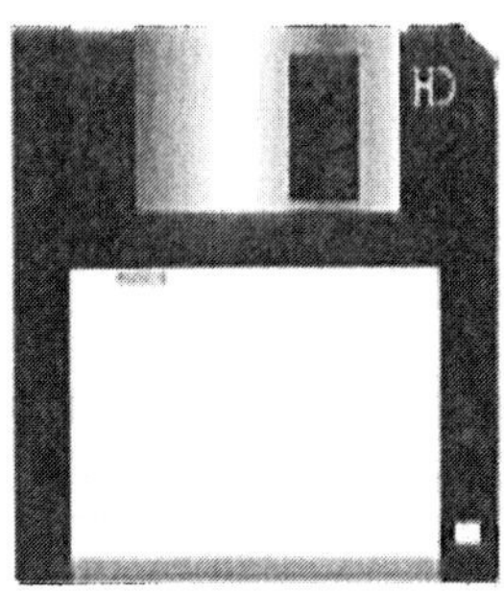

Floppy Disk

ZIP Disk

CD ROM

2. Communication devices

Communication devices are used to send and receive data from one computer to another. For example Modem, Network Interface Card, Hub, switches, routers, gateways and even networking cables are included in communication devices

Wireless PCI NIC Card

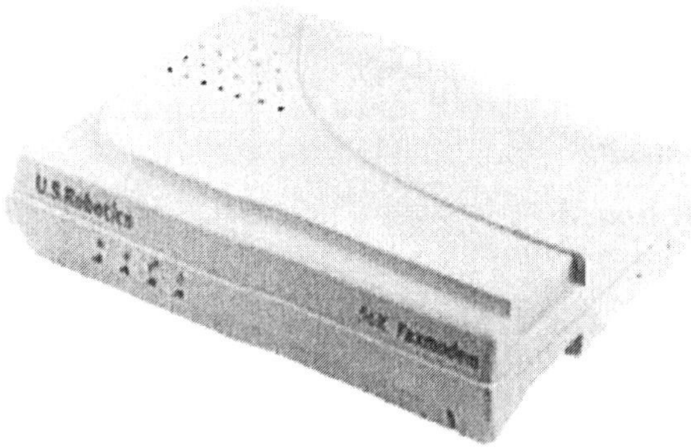

External Modem

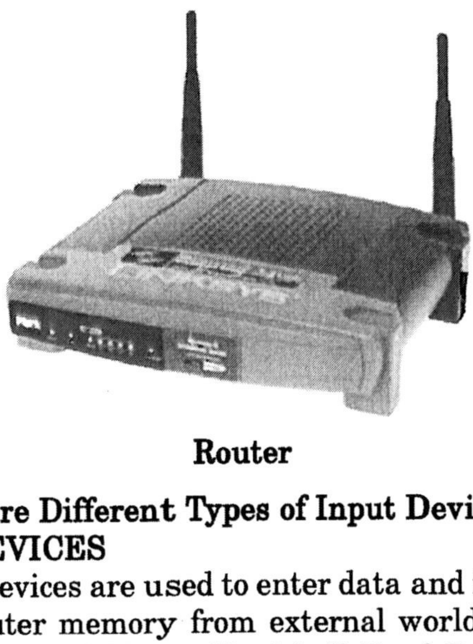

Router

2.2 What are Different Types of Input Devices

INPUT DEVICES

Input devices are used to enter data and instructions into computer memory from external world. Examples include: Keyboard, Mouse, Track ball, Track Pad, Joy stick, Touch Screen, Light pen, Touch Screen, Scanner, Digital Camera, Microphone, Graphics tablet. They perform three main functions

1. Receive data from user
2. Convert data into binary form [the language of 0 and 1 also called the machine language.

Machine language is the only language, a computer can understand directly.

3. Provide converted data to computer memory for processing

1. **Key board**

Keyboard is the most familiar input device. It is most widely used input device to enter data and instructions into the computer. Keyboard has a set of keys like a typewriter. It has alphabetic keys for A,B,C...Z or a,b,c,...z. It has numeric keys like 0,1,2,3,...9. It has function keys F1,F2,...F12 used to perform specific tasks.It has other keys used for editing like Delete, Backspace, Home, End, etc.

2. **Mouse**

Mouse is an input device used to control motion of pointer on screen. A mouse has two or three buttons called Left, Right and Middle button. Buttons are used to perform different functions. It has a rubber or metal ball inside its body. Mouse is rolled over a flat surface called mouse pad. The movement of ball is detected by internal circuits of mouse. These circuits convert this movement into digital signals, which are sent to computer. Mouse is used in graphical applications. It is also used for playing video games on computer.

3. Track Ball

Track Ball is an input device like a mouse. It is used in Lap top computers to control motion of pointer on screen. It is a pointing device like upside down mouse. It has a ball on its upper side. This ball is moved by fingers or thumb and the pointer moves accordinglyon screen.

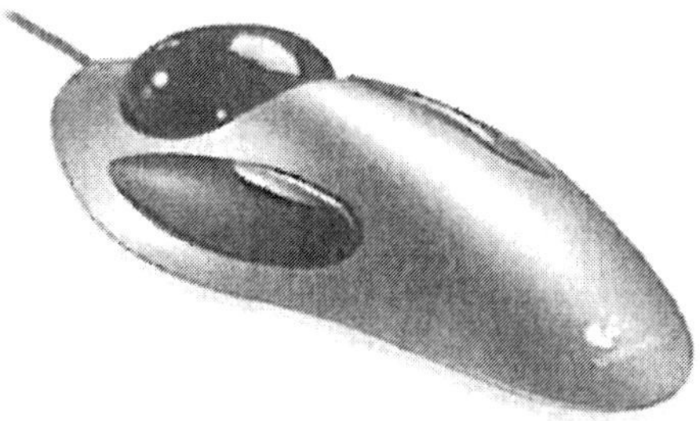

4. Track Pad

Track pad is a pointing input device. It is used in Lap top computers to control motion of pointer on screen. Track pad is a stationary input device. It has a flat surface of 1.5 to 2 square inch. Finger is moved on this surface to move pointer on screen.

5. Joy stick

Joystick is an input device used to play games on computer. It is used to control motion of an object quickly in game with the help of a hand held stick. This stick can be moved forward, backward or sideways. This stick is mounted on a ball. When stick is moved then ball is moved and signals are sent to the computer.

6. Light Pen

Light pen is an input device consisting of a special pen that is connected to a computer's monitor. The user points at the screen with the pen and selects items or chooses commands either by pressing a clip on the side of the light pen or by pressing the light pen against the surface of the screen (the equivalent of performing a mouse click).

7. Microphone

Microphone is an input device used to enter sounds into the computer. We can record sounds in computer with the help of microphone and sound card.

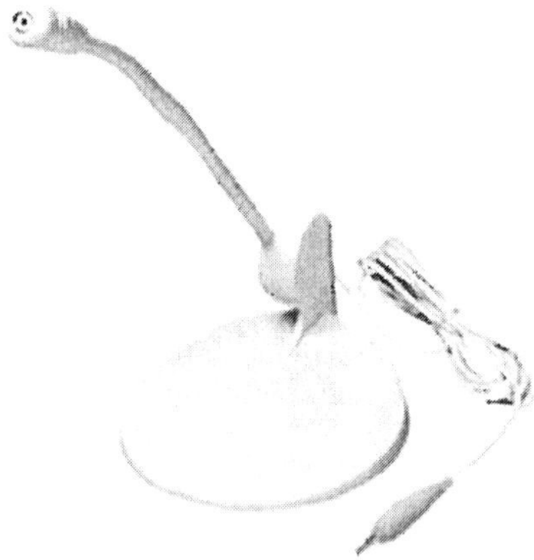

8. Scanner

Scanner is an input device. It is used to save pictures or text on paper into computer memory. It converts picture or text on paper in to binary form and saves it in computer memory. With the help of scanner we may save our time to type a lot of text. For example, if we have a book and wish to enter the whole text of book in to computer. It will be a long, tedious and time consuming job. But if we use a scanner, we can do this with in less time. We can scan each page of book. Editing of the scanned text is also possible. So our job will become very easy with the help of a scanner.

9. Graphics tablet / digitizer

A graphics tablet consists of a special pen called stylus and a flat pad. The image is created on the monitor screen as the user draws it on the pad with the help of stylus (special pen). Graphics tablet is also called a digitizer.

10. Touch Screen

In ATM and in latest smart phones, touch screen is used to receive input from the user. The user enters data by the touch of his finger on different menu options or icons present on touch screen.

11. Digital Camera

A digital camera is one of the latest input devices. We can take pictures with he help of digital camera. These pictures are saved on digital camera's internal memory. There is no need of a film role as used in traditional cameras. Later on we can easily input these pictures with the help of a data cable into computer's memory. Latest digital cameras can take still snapshots and can record video as well.

2.3 Explain Different Types of Output Devices

Outputdevices

Output devices are used to display results of processing to the user. They perform the following functions:

1. Receive results from memory
2. Convert data into human readable form
3. Display results to the user

Examples include: Monitor, printer, plotter, speaker, and multimedia projector.

1. Monitor

LCD Monitor

CRT Monitor

Monitor is the most commonly used output device used to display results of processing. It has a TV like shape. Pictures on monitor are formed with picture elements called PIXEL. Monitors may be Monochrome that will display results in Black & White. Color Monitors are also available. They display results in multi colors. Monitor produces soft copy output.

2. Printers

Printers are used to produce hard copy output. They print processing results on paper. Printers are divided into two main categories:

- Impact Printers
- Non-Impact printers

Impact Printers.

These printers print with striking of hammers or pins on ribbon. For example Dot Matrix printer and daisy wheel printers are impact printers.

Non-Impact Printers.

These printers do not use striking mechanism for printing. They use electrostatic and laser technology. Quality and speed of these printers is better than Impact printers. For example Laser printer and Inkjet printers are non-impact printers.

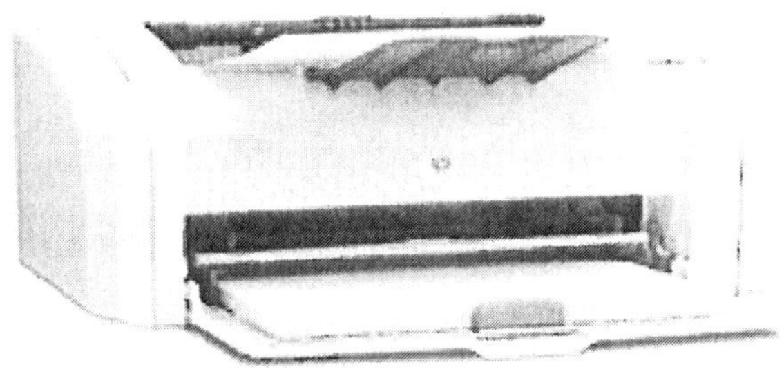

3. Speaker

Speakers for Desktop computer

Speaker produces sound output. We can listen recorded voices, sounds or music with the help of speaker. Speaker produces sound output with the help of sound card.

4. Plotter

Plotters are used to draw different designs of buildings or internal structure of machines. Mostly Engineers and Architects use plotters.

5. Multimedia Projector.

Multimedia Projector

Multimedia projector is used to produce computer output on a big screen. These are used in meeting rooms or in classrooms of educational institutes.

2.4 Explain Parts of CPU and its Working

Central Processing Unit / CPU / Microprocessor / Processor

Central processing unit is the brain of computer. It is also called CPU or processor. Processor is used to process data according to given instructions. It performs arithmetic and logical operations on data. It controls all activities of different parts of a computer. As brain in human body controls all other parts of body and takes decisions, CPU controls all other parts of the computer and their working. A CPU has three basic parts: Arithmetic Logic unit, Control unit and Registers.

Figure: Microprocessor or Processor or CPU or Central Processing Unit

1. ARITHMETIC LOGIC UNIT (ALU)

ALU performs data processing according to given instructions. All computations are done in this unit. ALU is the real place in computer where actual execution of instructions takes place. ALU may be further categorized into two sections according to their function:

ARITHMETIC SECTION of ALU performs arithmetic operations like addition, subtraction, multiplication and division on data.

LOGIC SECTION of ALU performs logical operations like comparison between two values. For example, 10>5 will give TRUE answer. And 5<1 will give FALSE answer. Control unit sends data and instruction to perform calculation on the data to the ALU. ALU then performs this calculation.

2. Control Unit

Control unit controls all over operations of different parts of computer. For example it takes data and instructions from input unit and stores it into memory. It sends data to ALU for processing. It takes results from ALU and sends it to output device. It can also store results in memory. Control unit performs all these functions by giving commands to relevant part of the computer. Control unit performs following four functions for executing instructions of a computer program.

1. Fetching: obtaining instruction from memory
2. Decoding: understanding this instruction
3. Data Fetching: If needed, obtaining data from memory
4. Executing: Control unit sends the instruction and data to ALU for taking suitable action on the instruction

3. Registers

A register is a very small and temporary memory area in ALU. It holds instruction and data as long as it is being processed by CPU. When instruction and data is fetched from memory then it is stored in a register. ALU contains a number of registers for example AX, BX, CX, DX etc. A Register may be of 8 bits, 16 bits, 32 bits or more.

2.5 What are Dual Devices or Both Input/ Output Devices

The devices that can be used to perform both functions -input and output- are called Dual Devices. These devices are also called Dual Purpose Devices or Both Input/Output Devices. With the help of a dual purpose device, we can enter data into computer as well as we can output data from the computer to outside world. For example, Dual devices include: Touch Screen Monitor, Modem, Network Interface Card, Sound card, Hard disk drive, Floppy disk Drive, Magnetic Tape Drive CD-Writer and DVD-Writer etc. These are also called Input/output devices, because they perform both functions.

Touch Screen Monitor

Touch Screen Monitor is an input/output device. It uses a special touch sensitive screen. The User can enter data by touching icons or menus on the screen. As soon as the user selects a command from menu, output is displayed on screen. Commonly touch screen monitors use sensors to detect touch of finger.

Modem

Internal modem

External modem

Modem stands for Modulator / Demodulator. Modem is a communication device. It performs two functions: Modulation (converting digital signal into digital signal) and Demodulation (converting analog signal to digital signal). It makes possible receiving data from internet into our computer (input) and sending data from our computer to another computer on internet (output). Modem sends and receives data from one computer to another through telephone lines. It links your personal computer to the Internet through your ISP (Internet Service Provider). A telephone line supports only analog signals, whereas computer accepts only digital signals. So when a computer wants to send data to another computer, digital data is converted into analog data before placing on telephone line. The process of converting digital signal into analog signal is called Modulation. Similarly, on the receiving computer, modem converts analog data (from telephone line) into digital data, before it is entered into receiving computer. The process of converting analog signal into digital signal is called Demodulation.

NIC - Network Interface Card

NIC or LAN card

NIC stands for Network Interface Card. It is used to link network computers for transmitting data. With the help of NIC our computer can receive data, instructions and information from another computer (input). NIC will also be helpful to send data from our computer to another computer on the network (output). NIC is also called a LAN card, local area network card or LAN adapter

Sound Card

Sound card or audio card

A sound card is a computer component that facilitates the input and output of audio signals to and from a computer. A speaker produces audio output with the help of sound card. In addition we use microphone to input our voice into computer with the help of sound card.

Hard disk Drive

Hard Disk Drive

Hard disk drive is an input/output device. It has read/ write heads to read data from hard disk (input) and to write data to hard disk (output).

Floppy disk Drive

Floppy disk drive is an input/output device. It has read/ write heads to read data from floppy disk (input) and to write data to floppy disk (output).

Magnetic Tape Drive

Magnetic Tape drive is an input/output device. It has read/write heads to read data from magnetic tape (input) and to write data to magnetic tape(output).

CD-Writer / CD-Recorder

CD-Writer is an input/output device. It is used to store data on CD. It is used to read data from CD(input) and to write data to CD(output).

DVD-Writer / DVD-Recorder

DVD-Writer is an input/output device. It is used to store data on DVD. It is used to read data from DVD(input) and to write data to DVD (output).

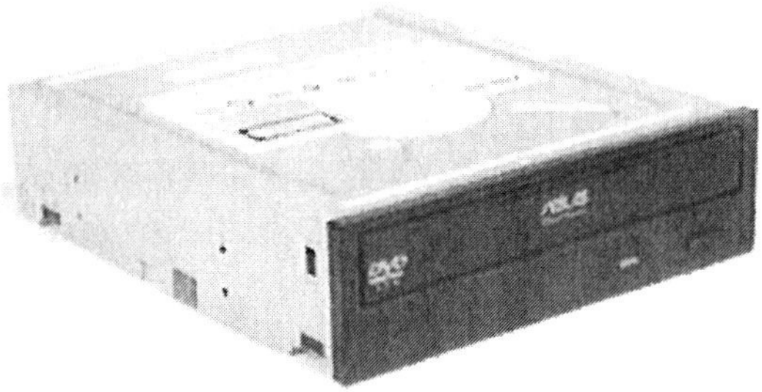

2.6 What is RAM, Explain Different Types of RAM

RAM

Ram stands for random Access Memory. Data in RAM can be accessed directly. That is, we can access data directly from any location of RAM in the same time. This Random Access quality makes RAM a very fast memory. RAM is volatile. Data and programs in RAM are erased when computer is turned off. Therefore RAM is a temporary memory. It is used to store those data and programs, which are currently being executed by CPU. Ram is also called Primary Memory or Main Memory.

Where RAM memory chip is installed?

RAM chip is installed into one of the memory slots on motherboard, as shown in the figure:

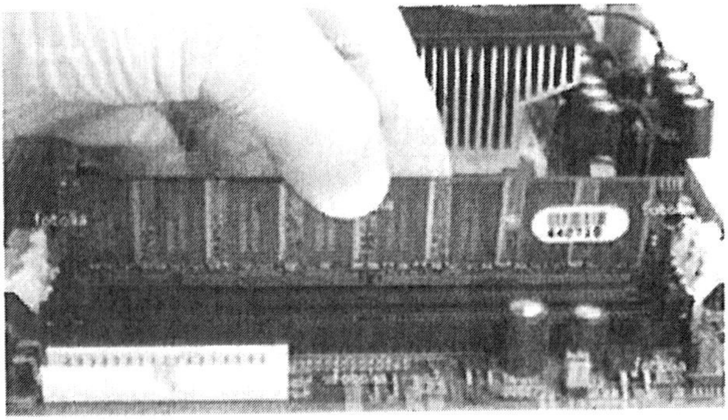

Importance of RAM.

1. A Program must be laoded in RAM for execution.

The programs and data currently being executed are in computer's main memory, that is, in RAM. The programs and data needed by these programs is loaded into RAM and run from this memory for FAST ACCESS. Because hard disk is very slow device, every program we run, is loaded into RAM from hard disk first, and then it is executed by processor. CPU is very fast device, it can take instructions and data to execute from RAM much faster than from a hard disk.

2. RAM is an Important Factor in increasing Speed of Computer

One of the most important factors affecting the speed and power of a computer is the AMOUNT OF RAM it has. Normally, the more RAM a computer has, the more speed and power of working it has.In fact, if a computer with a very fast processor has inadequate amount of RAM, it may still run slowly, especially when running multiple programs.

Types of Ram

There are two main types of Ram.

Dynamic Ram (DRAM)

Dynamic Ram is widely used in personal computers. It is a cheaper kind of RAM. DRAM loses electric charge with the passage of time, so DRAM needs to be refreshed frequently. Otherwise, it may lose data. Dram is recharged many times in a second. Therefore, it is slower than SRAM. Since CPU cannot access the data from DRAM while it is in the process of refreshing or recharging.

Static Ram (SRAM)

Static Ram does not need to be refreshed again and again. So processor can access data from static RAM faster than DRAM. There is no time wastage in refreshing the memory again and again. Static RAM is more expensive and faster than DRAM. Static Ram is used to build a very fast memory called CACHE (pronounces 'cash') memory.

2.7 What is ROM Explain Different Types of ROM

ROM

ROM stands for Read Only Memory, because its contents can be read and used only and we cannot change or delete its contents. It is a nonvolatile memory. Its retains its contents even after switching off the computer. Therefore, ROM does not require electricity to retain its contents. ROM is a permanent memory. The instructions in ROM are written at the time of manufacturing by the manufacturer.

Importance of ROM

1. One important reason a computer needs ROM is that instructions stored in ROM (called ROM BIOS - Basic Input/Output System)execute on start-up of computer and guide the computer what to do. They make the computer ready for work.

2. ROM contains a set of start-up instructions to check that memory is functioning well and check for other hardware devices.

3. These instructions also check for an operating system and load its necessary part into RAM; so that a user interfaces for example "Windows Desktop" is displayed on computer screen. Now computer is ready to work with. A user now can easily perform work on computer.

Where ROM Chip is installed?

ROM chip is fixed on motherboard as shown in the figure: AMIBIOS -American Megatrends ROM chip.

Picture of ROM fixed on mainboard

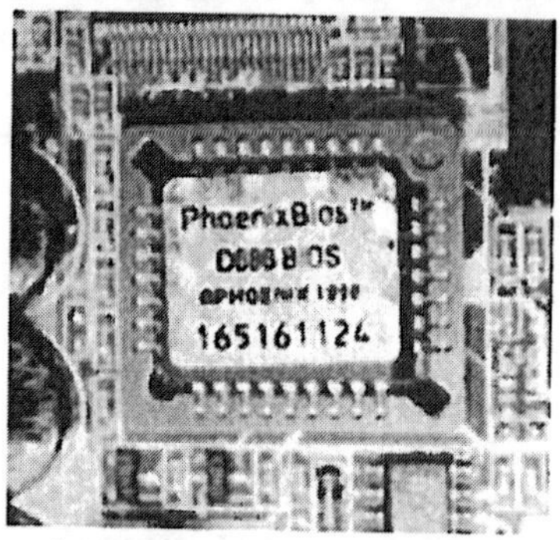

Another picture of Rom

Types of ROM

Following are the types of ROM

PROM

PROM stands for Programmable Read Only Memory. Instructions can be stored in PROM only once. Then it becomes ROM and we cannot change instructions in it. Initially PROM is a blank chip. Once instructions are written on it, then it became ROM. Now we cannot change or delete the instructions. If there is any error in writing instructions then PROM chip becomes unusable.

EPROM

EPROM stands for Erasable Programmable Read Only Memory. Program instructions written on EPROM can be erased and changed with the help of ultra violet rays. So if once we write instruction on this chip with errors, we can erase wrong instructions and rewrite new instructions.

EEPROM

EPROM stands for Electrically Erasable Programmable Read Only Memory. Program instructions written on EEPROM can be erased with the help of electricity and rewritten.

2.8 Discuss Differences Between RAM and ROM

We have already discussed the topics:

1. RAM and Types of RAM
2. ROM and Types of ROM

Here we discuss differences between RAM and ROM

Sr.	*RAM*	*ROM*
1.	RAM stands for Random Access Memory	ROM stands for Read Only Memory.
2.	RAM is a temporary memory.	ROM is a permanent memory.
3.	RAM is a volatile memory.	ROM is a nonvolatile memory.
4.	When computer is turned off, all data and programs are erased from RAM.	When computer is turned off, all data and programs are retained in ROM.
5.	RAM is a Read / Write memory. Data can be read and written to RAM.	ROM is a read only memory. Data from ROM only can be read and not written.
6.	Data and programs in RAM can be changed.	The contents of ROM cannot be changed.

(Contd.)

(Contd. Table)

Sr.	*RAM*	*ROM*
7.	Data or programs in RAM can be deleted.	Contents of ROM cannot be deleted.
8.	The instructions and data are written (loaded) in RAM at execution time, when computer is working.	The instructions in ROM are written at the time of manufacturing.
9.	RAM is used to load data and programs currently running.	ROM contains the instructions that help the computer to start-up and make it ready for work.
10.	RAM is much faster than ROM.	ROM is slower than RAM.
11.	RAM has two main types: Static RAM and Dynamic RAM	ROM has three types: PROM, EPROM and EEPROM
12.	Physically RAM chip is larger than ROM chip.	Physically ROM chip is smaller than RAM chip.
13.	Picture of RAM	Picture of ROM

2.9 Explain different types of storage devices

Storage Devices

Storage devices are used to store data and instructions permanently. Storage devices are also called secondary storage devices / backing storage devices / external storage devices or auxiliary storage devices. Examples of storage devices include Hard Disk, CD and DVD etc.

Why Secondary Storage Devices are Used?
Secondary storage devices are used because:

1. Primary memory (RAM) is volatile and temporary. When computer is switched off, all data in ram is erased.
2. Storage devices can store large amounts of data and instructions permanently whereas Primary memory has less capacity of storing data.

Types Of Storage Devices
There are three main types of storage devices:

1. Magnetic Tape 2. Magnetic Disk 3. Optical Disk

1. Magnetic Tape

Magnetic tape is the oldest storage device. It is made of plastic coated with magnetic material. Data is stored on magnetic tape in the form of magnetic spots. Tape drive is used to read and write data on tape. Magnetic disk is sequential access device. It is slower device than magnetic disk or optical disk. Magnetic tapes are used in reels of different lengths, for example 200, 600, 1200 feet etc.

2. Magnetic Disk

A magnetic disk is a thin circular metal or plastic disk coated with magnetic material. Data is stored in the form of magnetic spots. Magnetic disk is random access device. It is faster than magnetic tape. There are three main types of magnetic disk:

a. Hard Disk
b. Floppy Disk c. Zip Disk

a. Hard Disk

The hard disk is also called fixed disk. It consists of one or more metal plates. The plates are fixed in the drive. Metal plates are coated with magnetic material to store data. A motor rotates disks. There is also an access arm and read / write heads to read and write data on disks.

Following are major characteristics of hard disk:

- The storage capacity of hard disk is much greater than floppy disk.
- Now a days hard disks of size 40 GB, 80 GB or more are available.
- Hard disk is covered in a hard jacket and there are less chances of disk damage due to dust and mishandling.
- Now days Operating system and application programs are installed on hard disk.
- Before using a magnetic disk we use operating system to format the disk. Operating system divides the disk into circles called tracks. Each track is divided into pie-shaped areas called sectors. Data is stored in sectors. Each sector can store 512 bytes.

b. Floppy Disk

Floppy disk is a small plastic plate coated with magnetic material. Data is stored in magnetic spots. Main advantage of floppy disk is that it is used to transfer data from one computer to another. Floppy disk drive is used to read and write data on floppy disk.

Floppy disk is available in two sizes:

- 3 ½ INCH Floppy Disk

It is also called micro floppy disk. Its diameter is 3½ inch. It is covered in a hard plastic cover. Read/Write window is covered with a metal shutter. When disk is inserted into disk drive then shutter is automatically opened. It can be write protected by a notch. Storage capacity of micro floppy is 1.44 MB.

- 5¼Inch floppy disk.

It is a 5¼inch diameter plastic plate coated with magnetic material. Its storage capacity is 1.2 MB. It is not used in modern computers.

c. Zip Disk

Zip disk is similar to 3 ½ inch floppy disk. But it can store 100 MB or more data. Zip disk drive is used to read and write data on a zip disk.

3. Optical Disk

LASER technology is used to read and write data on Optical disk. LASER stands for Light Amplification through Emission of Radiation. Laser beam writes on the surface of optical disk by creating very small holes. The presence of hole represents a One and absence of the hole represents a Zero. There are following main types of optical disk.

1. CD-ROM, 2. CD-R or WORM, 3. CD-RW

4. DVD-ROM, 5. DVD-R, 6. DVD-RW

1. CD-ROM

CD-ROM stands for Compact Disk-Read Only Memory. The data stored on CD-ROM can only be read. It cannot be deleted or changed. It is a portable storage device. Data can be easily transferred by CD Rom from one computer to another. Commonly it can store 650 MB / 700 MB/ 750 MB data. It is used to store large amounts of data like Software or audio/video data. We purchase Software, movies, dramas, lectures, books, wallpapers and other data on CD-ROM.

2. CD-R (CD Recordable) Or WORM (Write Once Read Many)

CD-R stands for Compact Disk -Recordable. Initially, it is a blank disk. User can store data on it only once. This is why it is also called WORM (Write Once Read Many) disk too. Because we can write data on it only once and later we can read many times. The devices to store data on CD-R are called CD Writers or CD Burners. We can write data on CD-R only once, but can read data many times. Because of this write once read many qualities, CD-R is often known as WORM (write once read many).

3. CD-RW (CD Rewritable)

CD-RW stands for Compact Disk Rewritable. This is a special type of CD. User can write data on it, if there

is an error in writing data, he may erase the contents and rewrite again. CD-Writers are used to store data on CD-RW.

4. **DVD - Digital Video Disk (DVD-ROM)**
   DVD stands for Digital Video Disk. A laser beam with a short wave length is used to create very very small holes on the surface of disk. So there are much more tiny holes on the surface of DVD as compared to that of CD. Therefore, storage capacity of DVD is much larger than CD. It can store up to 17 GB or more data. DVD-ROM is prerecorded and it can contain data like movies, videos and software etc. User cannot change or delete data from DVD-ROM. It is read only.

5. **DVD-R (DVD-Recordable)**
   DVD-R stands for Digital Video Disk Recordable. Initially it is a blank disk. User can store data on disk

only once. Then it becomes read only. It is normally used to store high definition video movies. DVD-Writers are used to store data on DVD-R.

6. **DVD-RW (DVD Rewritable)**

   DVD-RW stands for Digital Video Disk Rewritable. User can write data on disk many times by erasing the old data.

2.10 What are Pointing Input Devices

A Pointing input device is an input device which is used to control the movement of the pointer to select items on a display screen. Examples of pointing devices include: Mouse, Track ball, Joystick, Pointing Stick, Graphic Tablet, Touch pad or Track pad, Touch Screen and Light pen etc.

1. **Mouse**

   Mouse is an input device used to control motion of pointer on screen. A mouse has two or three buttons

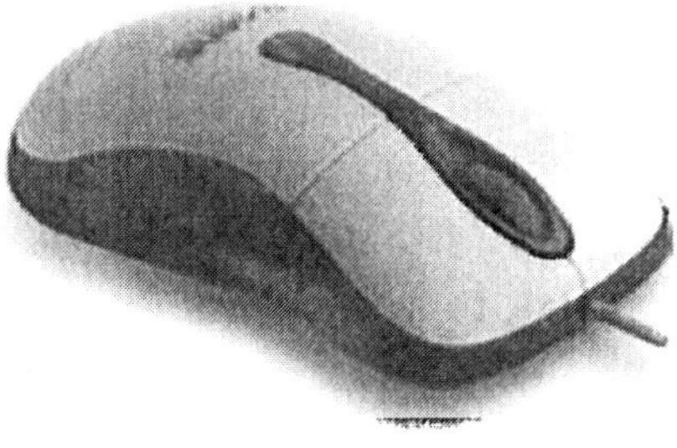

called Left, Right and Middle button. Buttons are used to perform different functions.

1. **Track Ball**

   Track Ball is an input device like a mouse. It is used in Lap top computers to control motion of pointer on screen. It is a pointing device like upside down mouse. It has a ball on its upper side. This ball is moved by fingers or thumb and the pointer moves accordingly on screen.

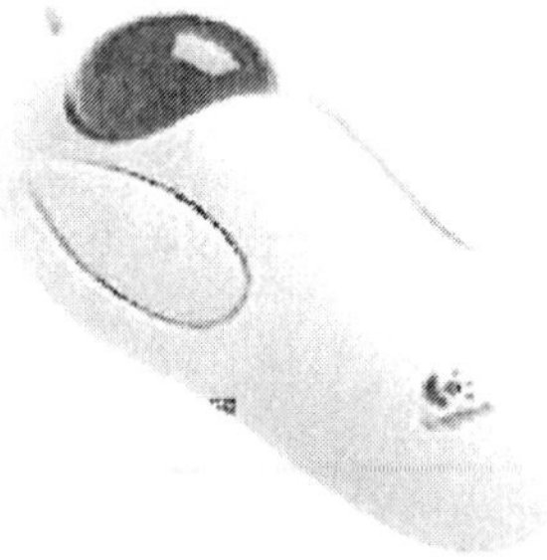

2. **Joystick**

   Joystick is an input device used to play games on computer.

4. **Pointing Stick**

   A pointing stick is a pressure sensitive small nub (similar to pencil eraser) used like a joystick. It is usually found on laptops fixed between the 'G', 'H', and

'B' keys. It operates by sensing the pushing force applied by the user. The pointer on the screen moves, when user pushes pointing stick with finger. Normally, it isused with laptop computers.

5. **Graphic Tablet**
   A graphics tablet consists of a special pen called stylus and a flat pad. The image is created on the monitor screen as the user draws it on the pad with the help of stylus (special pen).

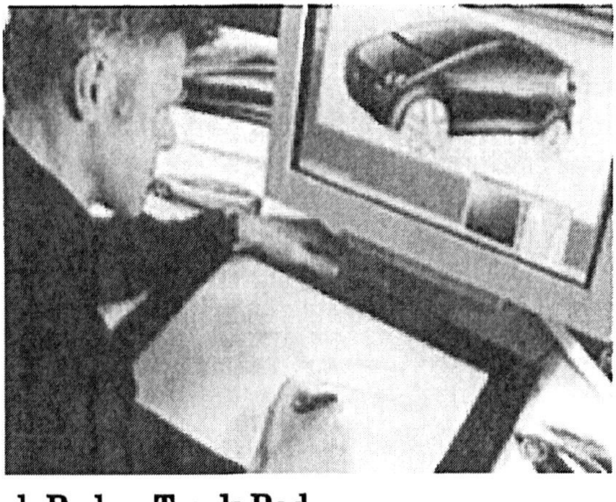

6. **Touch Pad or Track Pad**
   Touch pad or Track pad is a pointing input device. It is used in Lap top computers to control motion of pointer on screen. Track pad is a stationary input device. It

has a flat surface of 1.5 to 2 square inch. Finger is moved on this surface to move pointer on screen.

7. **Touch Screen**

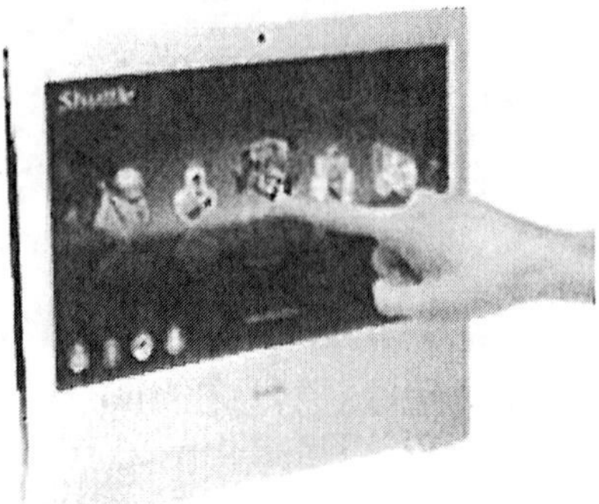

In ATM and in latest smart phones, touch screen is used to receive input from the user. The user enters data by the touch of his finger on different menu options or icons present on touch screen.

8. **Light Pen**

Light pen is an input device consisting of a special pen that is connected to a computer's monitor. The user points at the screen with the pen and selects items or chooses commands.

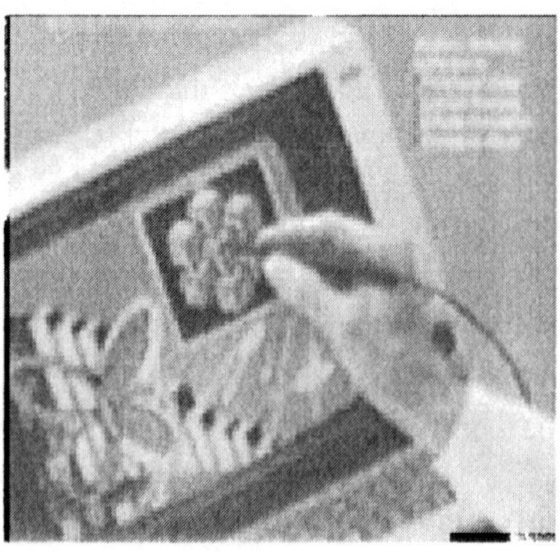

2.11 Different Types of Mouse Input Device

A mouse is a small, lightweight pointing input device. Mouse is moved on a flat surface to control the movement of the pointer on a screen. A mouse usually has two or three buttons. These buttons are used to perform different tasks.

Different types of mouse are as follows:

- **Mechanical Mouse**

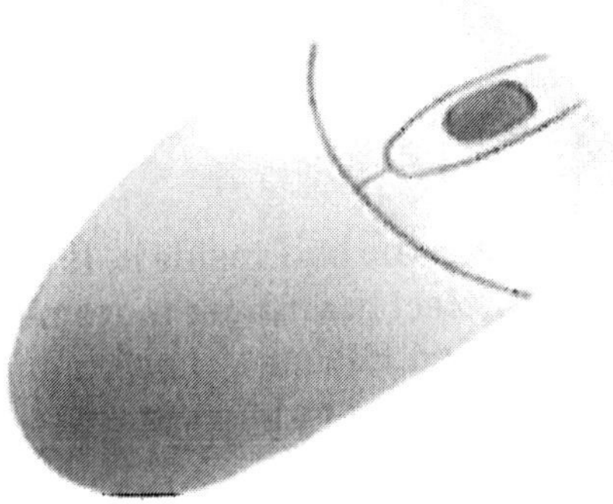

Mechanical mouse contains a rubber or metal ball inside it. The movement of the cursor depends on the movement of the ball.

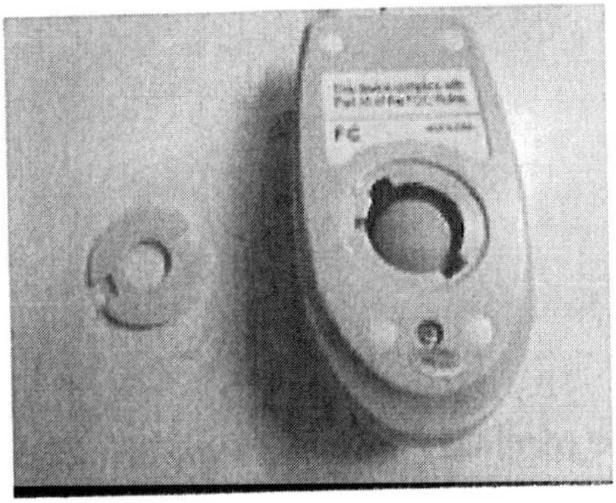

This mouse is normally used on mouse pad. Mouse pad is a- small flat pad made of rubber or foam to provide easy movement for the mouse. It protects the mouse from dust and dirt.

- **Optical Mouse**

Optical mouse contains no ball inside it. It uses a device that emits light to detect the mouse movement. Optical sensor or laser is used in these types of mouse. It is more expensive than mechanical mouse.

- **Wireless Mouse**

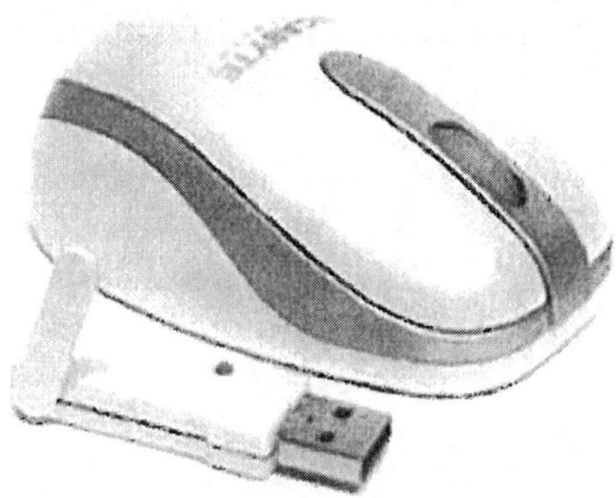

Wireless or cordless mouse is a type of mouse that does not require a wire to work. It transmits data using wireless technology like radio waves or infrared light waves. The receiver is connected to the computer through a serial or USB port.

2.12 Types Of Scanners Input Device

Scanner / Optical Scanner

A scanner is an input device for computer. It can scan any printed document with text as well as images. It will:

- Read any printed paper or picture,
- Convert text or images into digital form
- Saves this converted digital file into computer storage for later use

Uses of Optical Scanners

You can scan your documents or pictures to:

1. Store into computer memory.
2. To save lot of effort and time because if you type the whole text on printed page, it will take effort as well as time).
3. Show image or text on computer screen or on a multimedia projector's screen.
4. In addition, you can send this scanned document or image to your friends all over the world with the help of Internet & Email.
5. You can publish the scanned documents or images on your website or blog.
6. You can apply online and send the scanned images of your academic documents in any part of the world within minutes.
7. If your scanner supports OCR - Optical Character Recognition, you can scan a page with printed text and save it in an editable computer file. You can change or add more contents in this scanned file.

Types of Optical Scanners

There are different types of scanners:

1. Flat Bed Scanner

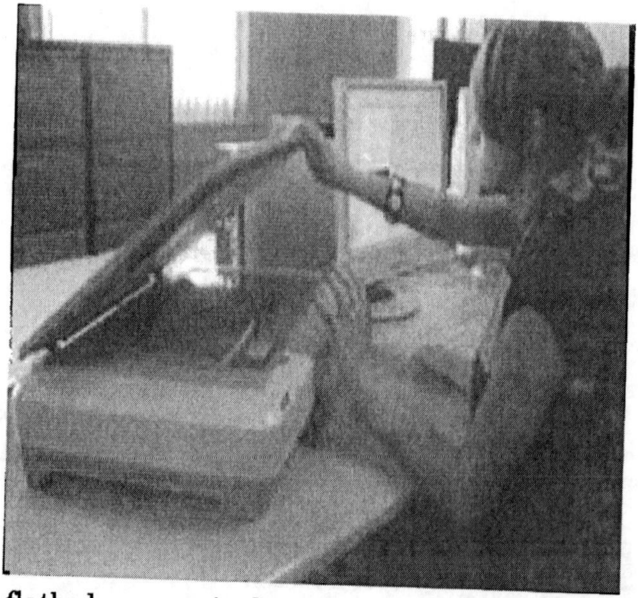

A flatbed scanner is the most common type of optical scanners used to scan printed text and images and save into computer storage as a digital file. It works on the principle of a photo copier machine. We pickup the cover of the scanner and place the printed page on the glass surface of the scanner. Now we will instruct scanner through computer software to start scanning. The scanner will scan with the help of light and save the digital file into computer storage. If you have an OCR scanner, you can save your text into editable form. This will save a lot of hard work and time to enter text by keyboard too. It is widely used in offices, schools, colleges, universities and homes for common scanning needs. If a book is very rare or difficult to find, we can scan it's all pages one by one. Later on we can take prints of these scanned pages through a color printer.

2. Sheet Fed Scanner

A sheet fed scanner works like a fax machine mechanism. In a sheet fed scanner, pages are entered into scanner like a fax machine.

Advantages of Sheet Fed Scanner

1. A feet shed scanner is relatively smaller in size.
2. It is more portable.
3. It takes less space.

Disadvantages Of Sheet Fed Scanner

1. It requires separate pages to scan. But, it cannot scan a book because of its binding.
2. It can scan normal papers with normal thickness only.

3. Hand Held Scanner

Hand Held scanner is a small, light weight scanner and portable scanner. It is used to scan small amount of data like short articles from news papers. It is held in hand and is moved over the text page or image slowly and smoothly from start to end. Its scan quality may be lower than flat bed or sheet fed scanner but it can used to capture small amounts of text or small images, quickly.

SkyPix Hand held Scanner

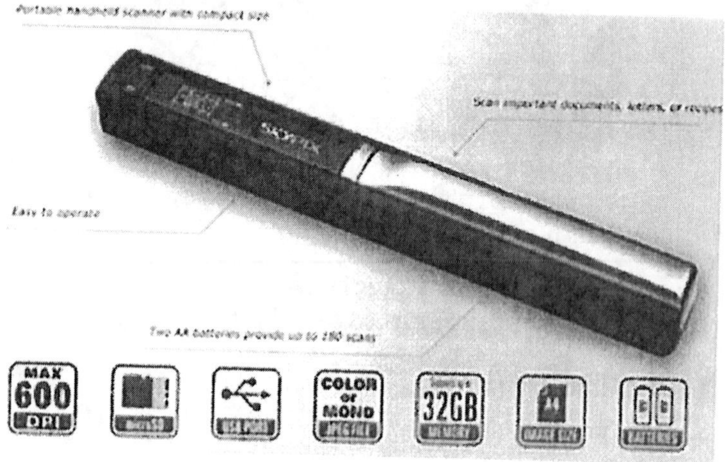

This is a portable, cordless hand held scanner that is used to scan and save important documents, letters, or pictures. It records scanned documents in its memory card. You can transfer these scanned documents on your computer for later use. You can scan and save important news from the newspapers or interesting articles from magazines.

4. **Drum Scanners**

   Drum scanners are used by the Publishers to scan images with details. Drum scanners use photomultiplier tube technology. In drum scanners, the document to be scanned is mounted on a glass cylinder. At the center of the cylinder is a sensor that splits

light bounced from the document into three beams. Each beam is sent through a color filter into a photomultiplier tube where the light is changed into an electrical signal. And in this way a complete image with immense details can be obtained. Drum scanners are widely used in publishing industry.

3

Computer Software

3.1 Explain Computer Software with Examples

Software

Software is a set of instructions that tell a computer what to do. Software is the set of instructions given to computer to perform a task or to control operations of computer. Software cannot be touched. The hardware cannot perform any task without software. Software is installed on hard disk. When we use any software it is loaded into RAM from hard disk.

Examples of software are:

1. MS Word
2. MS EXCEL
3. MS POWER POINT,
4. WinZip
5. Norton Anti-Virus
6. MSN Messenger
7. and MS Windows etc.

Microsoft WORD:

MS Word

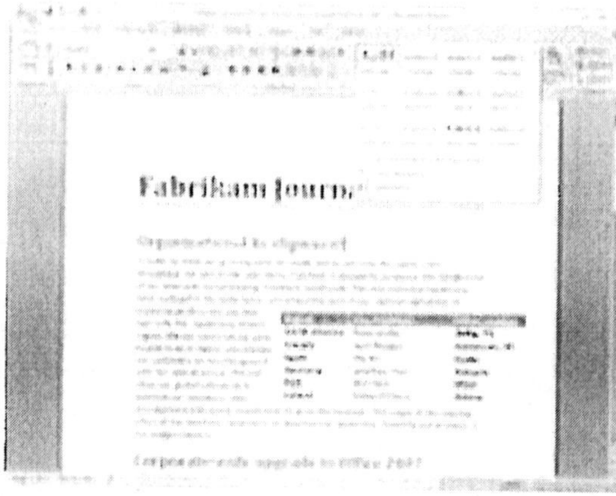

This software is used to prepare letters, applications, office documents and all types of documents and books etc.

Microsoft Excel:

MS Excel

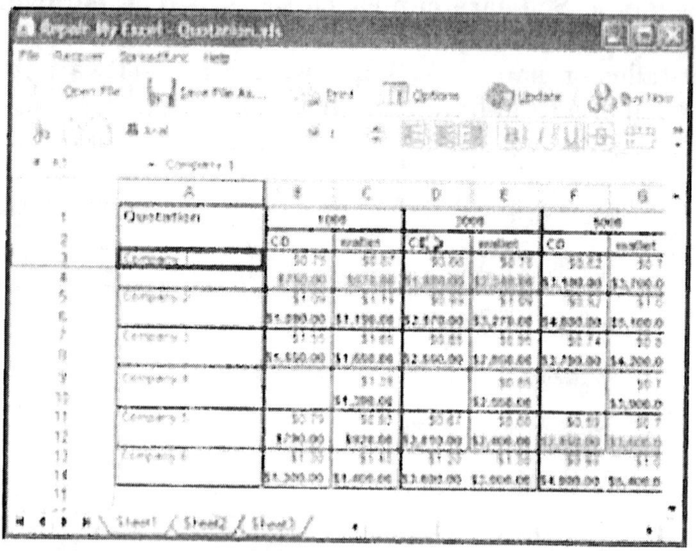

It is used calculations and preparing electronic worksheets for example creating Employees Pay Sheet or Students Result Sheet.

MS POWER POINT:

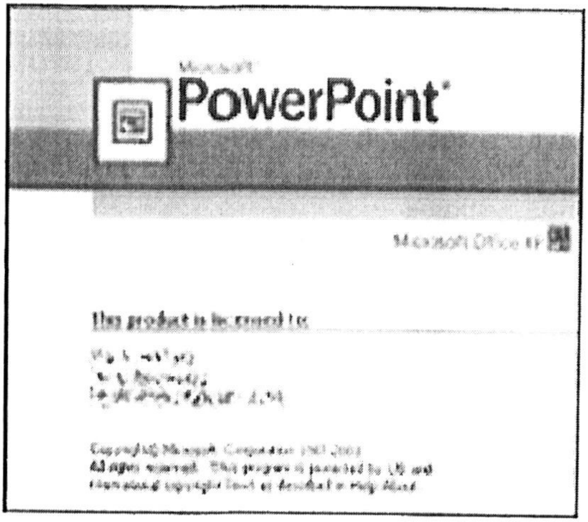

It is used to prepare presentations to be presented on multimedia projectors.

WinZip:

This software is used to store a file as compactly as possible, in the minimum file size possible. WinZip makes easy to take files from one computer to another and stores them in less storage space. When we need to use the zipped file, we have to unzip it or extract it to the original state and size.

Norton Anti-Virus:

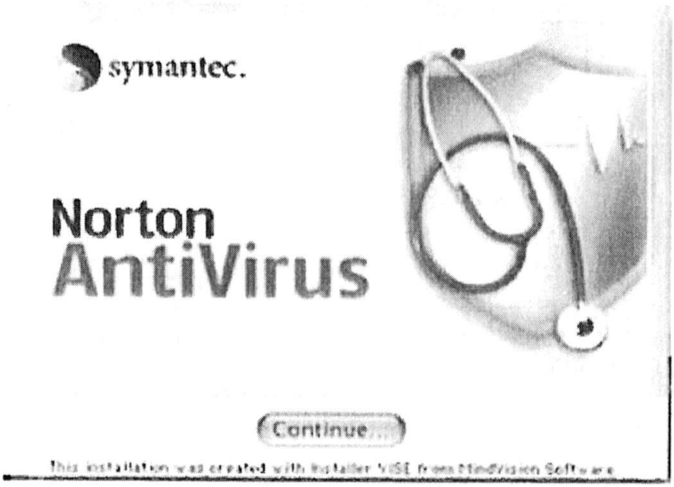

This software is used to detect and remove virus attacks on your computer.

MSN Messenger:

It is used for online chatting with friends all over the world.

MS Windows:

Microsoft Windows is the most popular Operating system in the world. First of all, you have to install an operating system on computer, before it will be ready for work. After installing the operating system like Microsoft Windows, now you can install application software like MS Excel, MS Word or games etc. In short, without an operating system you cannot use a computer.

3.2 Explain Different Types of Software
Types of Software

The main types of software are **system software** and **application software**.

1. System Software

System software is a set of programs to implement certain functions in a computer system. It controls the overall operations and components of a computer system.

It is the base on which application programs are executed. It is an interface between user and computer. Operating systems like Windows, Linux and UNIX are the main example of system software. Similarly device driver's software are also examples of system software.

Examples of system software are as follows:

- **Operating Systems**
  Operating system is software to control overall operations and components of a computer system. e.g., Windows, UNIX, Linux and Dos etc.

- **Utility Programs**
  Utility program is used to solve a particular problem of software or hardware, for example, Antivirus program, disk scanner and File Viewer etc.

- **Device Drivers**
  Device driver is software that permits a computer system to communicate with a device. e.g., device driver software for a modem comes with it on CD. We have to install device driver before using a device.

- **Language Processors**
  Language processor is software that converts a source program into object program. For example C- complier converts a program written in C language into object program (machine code).

2. **Application Software**

Application software is a program needed to perform various applications on the computer by the user. It helps a computer user to solve specific problems like to prepare letters and other documents, to create pictures and advertisements, to perform large calculations quickly etc.

The application software runs on top of the operating system software.

Examples of application software are as follows:

(i) **Word Processing**

Word processing software is used to produce letters, applications and other documents. Microsoft Word is the most popular application software used for word processing.

(ii) **Spreadsheets**

Spreadsheet program is used to create electronic worksheets. These worksheets are used to perform calculations on large amounts of data quickly and automatically. Microsoft Excel is a popular spreadsheet program.

(iii) **Databases**

Database software is used to record data of an organization on computer in compact and efficient form. MS Access, MS SQL Server and Oracle are examples of database software.

(iv) **Graphics**

Graphics software is used to produce advertisements, posters and pictures etc. for example CorelDraw and Photoshop are popular graphics software.

(v) **Communication**

Communications software is used to communicate with different people using Internet, e.g., MSN Messenger, yahoo messenger and Internet Explorer.

3.3 System Software and Application Software: Differences

Q. Differentiate between system software and application software

System Software:

System software is a set of programs to control all components of computer and to manage overall operations of computer system. System software is used as a base to install and run all application software. Examples of system software include:

1. Operating Systems, like Microsoft Windows, DOS, Unix and Linux
2. Device Drivers like Device driver software of a Printer (found on CD normally provided with the printer)
3. Utility Programs like AVAST anti-virus, Disk Scanners and File Viewers etc.

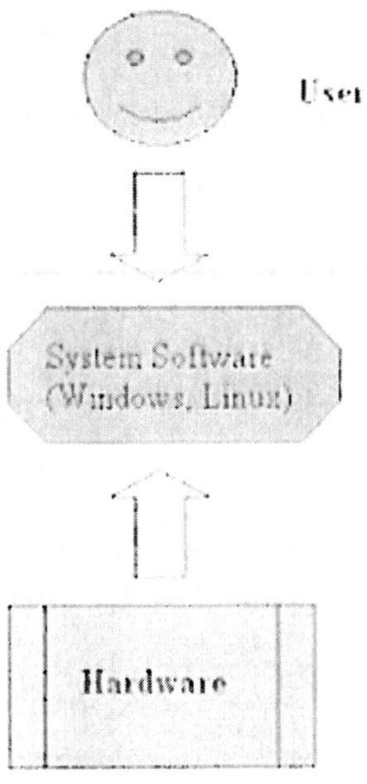

Application Software:

Users can use Application Software to perform different applications on computer. Application Software generally performs a specific task for a computer user. Examples of Application software include:

1. Word processors like Microsoft Word
2. Spreadsheet Software like MS Excel
3. Database software like Microsoft Access etc.

Difference between System & Application Software

System Software	*Application Software*
1. It is a set of programs to control computer components and operations.	1. It is used to solve particular problems of user.
2. It is general-purpose software.	2. It is specific purpose software.
3. It executes all the time in computer. Because it controls overall operations and components of computer.	3. It executes as and when required. For example, if we need to write a letter, we will open Microsoft Word - an application software. And after we have written and printed the letter, we will close Microsoft Word.
4. The number of system software is less than application software.	4. The number of application software is much more than system software.
5. System software is essential for a computer to work. Without System software (like operating systems), a computer is useless. We cannot use computer hardware with-out system software. That is why we install an operating system first of all, after buying a new computer.	5. Application software is not essential for a computer to work. For example, if we need to play some games then we buy a game CD or download games from internet, and install in our computer.
6. Examples are: Windows, Dos, Unix, Linux, Norton Antivirus etc.	6. Examples are: MS Word, MS Excel, MS Power point etc.

3.4 Customized and Packaged Software

Q. Explain Customized software and packaged software.

(a) Customized Software

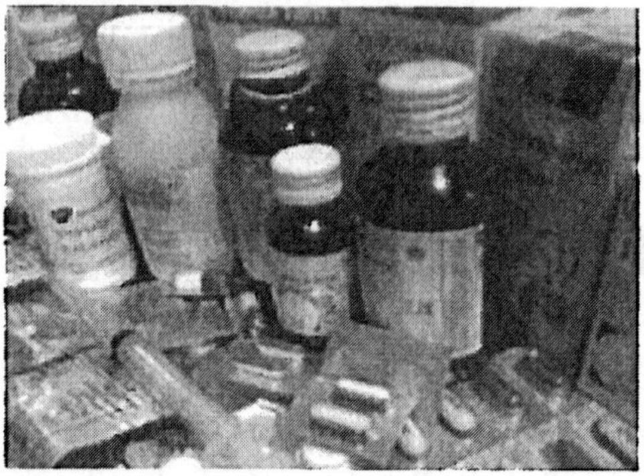

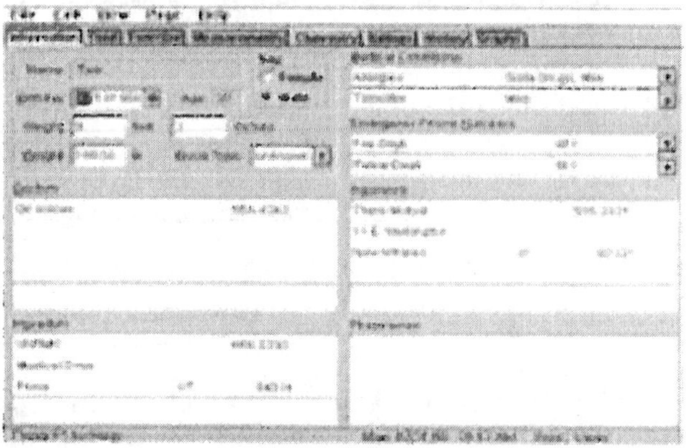

Customized software is a type of application software that is designed for a particular customer or organization. When packaged software does not fulfill needs of an organization then a programmer / software developer / software engineer is hired. The programmer will develop needed custom software for that organization according to the organizations specific needs and requirements. Student Information software developed for Govt. Post Graduate College of Commerce, Rahim Yar Khan is an example of customized software. It will be used to store all related data about students, admissions and examinations etc.

(b) Packaged Software

Packaged software is a type of application software that is developed for sale to the general public. It is also known as off-the-shelf software or Pre-Written software. It facilitates thepeopleto perform day-to-day activities. Examples of packaged software are word processing software and spread sheet software.

For example, Microsoft Office is packaged software. Microsoft Office ia set of different application software like Microsoft Word, Microsoft Excel, Microsoft Access and Microsoft Power Point.

4

Data, Data Processing, Information

4.1 Define Data and Information with Examples

DATA

Data is the collection of raw facts and figures. It is without any proper meaning.

Data may be collection of words, numbers, graphics or sounds.

Examples of Data

1. **Student Data on Admission Forms**
   When students get admission in a college. They fill admission form. This form contains raw facts (data of student) like name, father's name, address of student etc.

2. **Data of Citizens**
   During census, data of all citizens is collected.

3. **Survey Data**
   Different companies collect data by survey to know the opinion of people about their product.

4. **Students Examination data**
   In examination data about obtained marks of different subjects for all students is collected.

Information

Processed data is called information. When raw facts and figures are processed and arranged in some order then they become information. Information has proper meanings. Information is useful in decision-making. Actually we process data to convert it into information.

Examples of Information:

1. **Student Address Labels**
   Stored data of students can be used to print address labels of students.

2. **Census Report (Total population, Literacy Rate, Male / Female ratio etc.)**
   Census data is used to get report/information about total population of a country and literacy rate etc.

3. **Survey Reports and Results**
   Survey data is summarized into reports/information to present to management of the company.

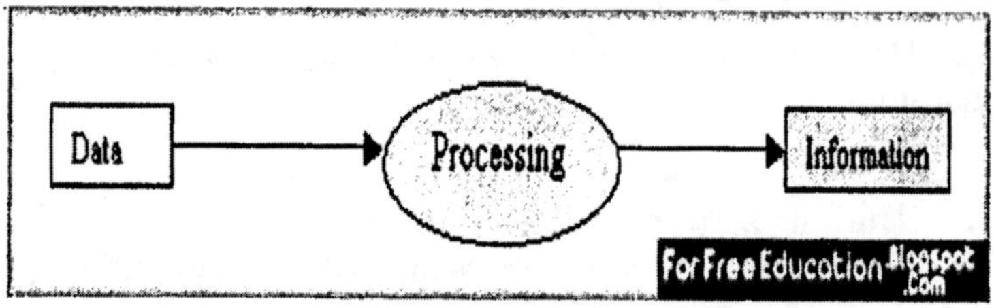

4. Result Cards of Individual Students, Result sheets of a particular Class In examination system collected data (obtained marks in each subject) is processed to get total obtained marks of a student. Total obtained marks are Information. It is also used to prepare result card of a student.

5. Merit List
   After collecting admission forms from candidates, merit is calculated on the basis of obtained marks of each candidate. Normally, percentage of marks obtained is calculated for each candidate. Now all the candidates' names are arranged in descending order by percentage.

This makes a merit list. Merit list is used to decide whether a candidate will get admission in the college or not.

4.2 Differences between Data and Information

Here we are going to discuss the differences between two typical terms of information technology: Data and Information. Data is a collection of raw facts and figures about an entity. Data may consist of numbers, characters, audio, video or pictures etc. When these data is processed according to requirements, then it is transformed into INFORMATION.

For example, consider Admission system of a Computer College. The candidates will submit admissions forms filled by them. Now all the facts and figures and picture of candidate on form is called data. These data may consist of name, father's name, date of birth, marks obtained, total marks, address, contact number and a latest photo graph of the candidate. Now the concerned person in the college office will process these data to prepare a merit list. He may calculate percentage of obtained marks of each candidate and arrange the records in descending order by percentage. This merit list is an example of Information. Information is useful in decision making. The merit list will declare the names of students who will have a right to get admission in the college.

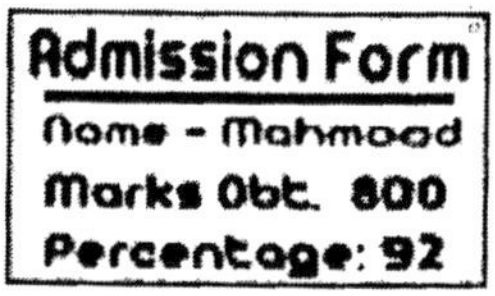

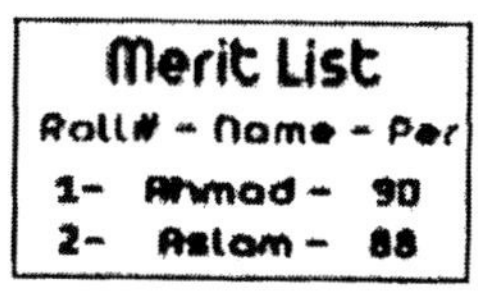

	DATA	*INFORMATION*
1	Data is collection of raw facts and figures.	Information isprocessed data.
2	Data is unarranged and unorganized.	Information is arranged and organized.

(Contd.)

(Contd.)

	DATA	INFORMATION
3	Datais un-meaningful.	Informationis meaningful.
4	Data is input.	Information is output.
5	Data is used less frequently.	Information is used frequently.
6	Data represents facts before processing.	Information represents results (obtained after processing).
7	Data is not helpful indecision-making.	Information is helpful in decision-making.
8	Data is raw material for information.	Information is the final product of data.
9	Data are unprocessed records	Information contains processed records
10	Data is in large amounts	Information is in small amounts
11	If data is lost, it is very difficult (or even impossible in some situations) to recollect.	If information is lost,it is easily derived from stored data, again.
12	Data is collected by observations,recordings, interview or survey etc. For example, if werecord the temperature of each hour recorded in a particular day is called temperature data.	Now we will processthese temperatures data to find useful information. For example if wearrange temperatures in ascending order, then we will find the information like:Minimum Temperature ofthe day= 15 C and Maximum Temper-ature of the day = 25 C.
13	Data is the asset of an organization and is not available for sale to public.	Normally, informationis available for sale to general public.

(Contd. Table)

(Contd.)

DATA	INFORMATION
14. Data depends upon the sources for collecting data, the collec-tion method sadopted and the people who will collect data.	Information depends

4.3 Explain Data Processing Cycle

After collecting data, it is processed to convert into information. The data is processed again and again until accurate result is achieved. This is called data processing cycle.

Data processing cycle involves following three basic activities:

1. **Input**
2. **Processing**
3. **Output**

1. INPUT

It is the process in which collected data is given to computer after converting into binary form. Input step can be further divided into following steps:

(i) Planning
Here objectives of data processing are defined. For example, in examination system, objective is to process student examination data to get result cards.

(ii) Data Collecting
Here data is collected. Data is the raw material for data processing. This must be accurate for getting accurate results.

(iii)Input
Here data is entered into computer.

(iv) Verification

Here collected data is verified to determine whether it is valid for processing. For example marks must be in numeric form.

(v) Coding

Data is stored in computer in binary form. Here data is converted (or coded) into computer readable (binary) form.

2. **PROCESSING**

Now data is ready for processing. We process collected data to convert into information. Some important activities in processing are as following:

(i) Data Classification

Here data is classified into different groups or sub-groups. So that it can be handled easily and separately. For example if we collect data about students of a college we will divide them into D.Com and B.Com class groups.

(ii) Data Sorting

Here data is arranged in some order. So that it can be accessed quickly. For example we can sort student data by Roll number or name.

(iii)Data Calculation/Processing

Here arithmetic and logical operations are performed on data to get the required result. For example total marks of each student are calculated.

3. **OUTPUT**

After completing the processing, output is received. Output step involves following steps:

(i) Testing

The results are tested to find if they are according to requirements. And any errors are removed. If results are not satisfactory then we repeat above-mentioned steps again and again until the accurate results are found.

(ii) Summarizing
Huge results are summarized to make them short and precise.

(iii) Storing results
The results are stored properly on secondary storage devices for future use.

(iv) Output the result
Here output is produced as softcopy on screen or as hard copy as printout. Information is sent to different places as needed.

(v) Feed Back
In this step we take comments from users about output results. If results are not satisfactory then we repeat above-mentioned steps again and again until the accurate results are found.

4.4 Types of Data Processing

DATA PROCESSING

Data processing is the sequence of operations performed on data to convert it into useful information. These operations may be arithmetic, statistical or logical operations. We can arrange or classify data. We can send and receive data from one point to another.

TYPES OF DATA PROCESSING (OR) LEVELS OF DATA PROCESSING)

There are three types of data processing.

(1) Manual data processing

(2) Mechanical data processing

(3) Electronic data processing

(1) Manual data processing

In manual data processing data is processed manually. No machine or tool is used.

All the calculations on data are performed manually. This is a slow method and errors may occur. This is an old

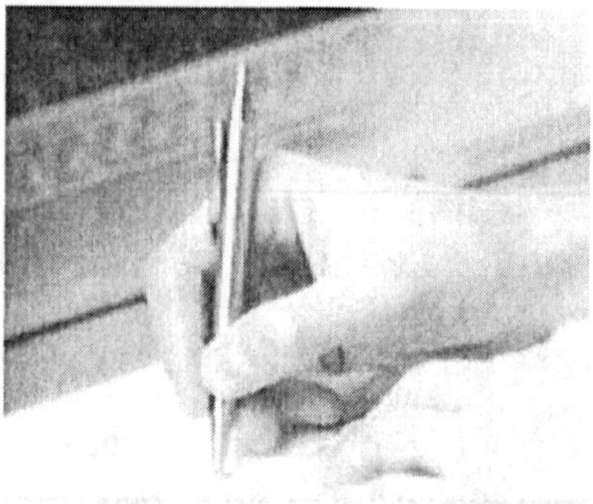

method. It was used before the invention of calculators. But data is still processed manually in many small shops.

Example: A book seller (a small book shop) records his daily transactions manually. He prepares bills by pen, paper and carbon paper (no doubt, brain is the main data processor in this case). At the end of day he will use carbon copies made on a particular date to know how many books he sold and how much income he got.

(2) Mechanical Data Processing

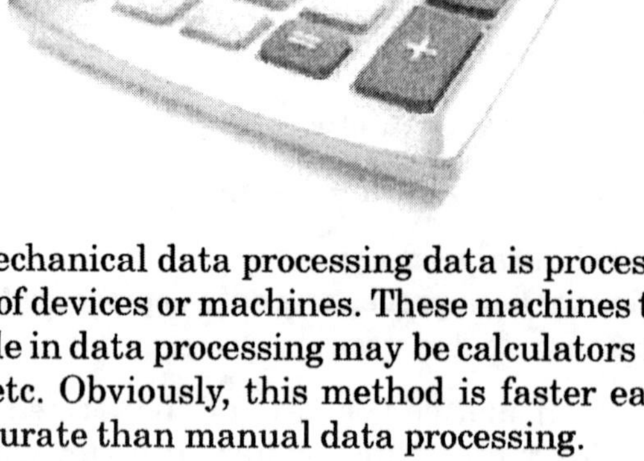

In mechanical data processing data is processed with the help of devices or machines. These machines that help the people in data processing may be calculators and type writers etc. Obviously, this method is faster easier and more accurate than manual data processing.

Example: Book seller can use a calculator to speed up his data processing system. There will be a less chance of errors in calculations. Bill calculations will be much faster with a calculator and easier too.

4.5 Electronic data processing

It is the latest and fastest method of data processing. Data is processed with the help of computer. First of all, data and set of instructions are given to the computer. Computer gives output results after processing the data according to instructions. This method of data processing is very fast and accurate. Electronic data processing is used in banks and business firms, Government offices, colleges, schools, universities, businesses and other institutes. Electronic data processing is being used in almost every field of life. Example:Suppose there are 800

students in a college. There is a manual library system in this college. If we want to know which students have not returned books since one year? We will have to search registers for 800 students' record. But computer can do this job within seconds.

In short, we can say that: Electronic data processing:

(i) is more fast

(ii) is less time consuming

(iii) can process large amounts of data easily

(iv) can present information in more attractive way

(v) will give 100 % error free results, if input and instructions are accurate.

5

Internet

5.1 Explain Internet and History of Internet

INTERNET

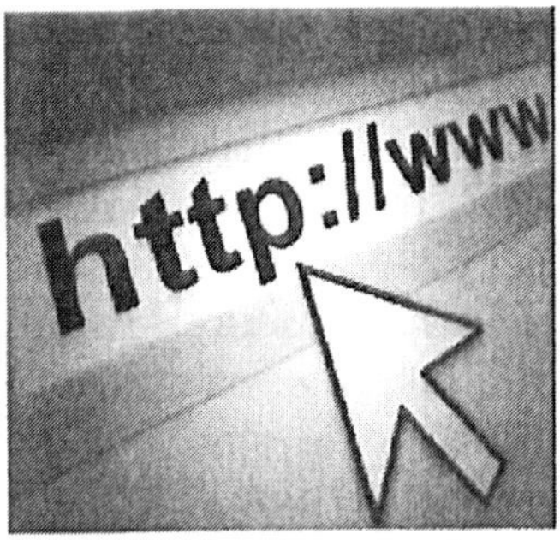

Internet is the network of networks around the world. It is made up of thousands of smaller networks. It is a global communication system. We can send and receive information from a city or country to another through Internet.

Main components of Internet are computers, communication media and modem etc. Modem is used to send and receive information though telephone lines.

Internet provides following main facilities:

- E- mail
- Chat
- Searching jobs

- Advertising for business
- E-commerce
- Searching information

To use Internet we must have

- Suitable computer
- telephone line
- modem
- web browser (for example, internet explorer)
- Internet connection or scratch card of an ISP

HISTORY OF INTERNET

(1) ARPANET

The seeds of internet were planted in 1969 by Advanced Research Projects Agency (ARPA) of US department of Defense. ARPA began to connect computers at different universities and defense contractors. This network was named ARPANET. The goal of ARPANET was to create a large network using telephone lines that could survive a nuclear attack or earthquake. Secondly, It also linked researchers at remote places to share the research work. ARPANET continued to develop through the 70s. Before the 80s there were fewer than 100 sites on the e Internet.

(2) NSFNET

In 80s US defense department stopped funding the ARPANET. In the mid-80s the National Science Foundation (NSF) joined the project. NSF developed the network to connect supercomputer centers in the US.

ARPANET was unable to handle rapidly increasing load of users. So NSF developed a new and higher capacity network called NSFNET.

(3) INTERNET

At this point many colleges and universities were encouraged to connect to the network. The number of sites began to increase rapidly. There were more than 100,000 sites in 1989. Similar networks were established in other countries in the world. The ARPANET, NSFNET and other networks were interconnected. The process of connecting different networks together is called INTERNET-WORKING. So this worldwide network of networks was named as INTERNET.

(4) Internet Backbones

NSFNET provided internet connections for academic research. But NSFNET did not permit users to do private business on internet. Therefore, many telecommunication companies created their own network backbones. Network back bones consist of high-speed data lines to carry huge volume of traffic. Local networks connect to these backbones.

In 1990 ARPANET was shut down. In 1995, government funding for NSFNET was discontinued. So commercial internet back bone services replaced them.

(5) Business on Internet

In the early 90s businesses were allowed on the internet.

(6) Internet Service providers

Since 1996, most of the internet traffic is carried by independent Internet Service Providers. Now at a very low cost, computers of offices, homes, institutes, hotels and net cafes etc can be connected to internet.

5.2 Services of Internet

Services Provided by Internet

Important services provided by internet are as the following:

1. The World Wide Web

This is also called web or www or 3w. The collection of all web pages in all web sites on Internet is called www. These web pages provide us information in the form of text, pictures, audio and video formats etc.

2. E-MAIL

E-mail stands for electronic mail. It is the most popular, cheap, easy and fastest mailing service. We can send and receive messages on internet with in seconds or minutes.

3. E-mail Discussion Groups

These are used to discuss different topics with other people by email.

4. Newsgroups

Newsgroups are discussion groups on internet. They are used for free exchange of information. A user sends a message to the news group site. Other users read this message from this site and reply. Newsgroups are provided by special computers called news servers.

5. Ecommerce

It stands for Electronic Commerce. E-commerce means to carry out business dealings by internet. Examples of Ecommerce include:

Online Banking, Online shopping and online education etc.

6. FTP

FTP stands for file transfer protocol. It is used to transfer files on internet easily and quickly. Audio, video, graphics and data files can be uploaded and downloaded using FTP.

7. Telnet

This program is used to access a remote computer on internet. You can access data and files from connected computer by Telnet. Telnet may also provide you a user interface on screen. You will give commands to remote computer by this user interface.

8. Chat

It is the most popular services by which two or more users can live chat with each other. We can chat by text or audio or video. Voice chat is just like talking on telephone.

Messenger software like Yahoo messenger or MSN messenger is used for chatting.

9. Gopher

A gopher on the Internet is a system for users to search for files via menus or directory structures. It uses plain English names and is text based only.

5.3 Advantages / Disadvantages Of Internet

ADVANTAGES OF INTERNET

Following are the main advantages of internet:

1. The World Wide Web

This is also called web or www or 3w. The collection of all web pages in all web sites on internet is called www. These web pages provide us information.

2. E-MAIL

E-mail stands for electronic mail. It is the most popular, cheap, easy and fastest mailing service. We can send and receive messages on internet with in seconds or minutes.

3. Newsgroups

Newsgroups are discussion groups on internet. They are used for free exchange of information.

4. Mailing Lists

Mailing lists provide information to the users on the selected topics through email. Mailing lists are maintained by different companies.

5. Online Banking

Several banks are online now. So we can manage our bank accounts on internet. Due to online banking, money is transferred from one city or country to another within seconds or minutes.

6. E-Commerce

E-commerce means the electronic commerce. It means that doing business on internet. Now we can sell and purchase goods from anywhere in the world through internet.

7. Job Search

You can search jobs on internet. There are many job seeking sites on internet.

8. Search Engine

Internet contains a very large amount of information. Search engine is used to easily and quickly find the required information. Many sites provide facility of search engine like Google, Yahoo, Find, Lycos and AltaVista.

9. Chat

It is the most popular services by which two users can live chat with each other. It is just like talking on telephone. We can chat by text or audio or video. Messenger software like Yahoo messenger or MSN messenger is used for chatting.

10. Internet Phone

We can call on phone to someone on internet. This is cheaper than calling by ordinary phone.

11. Fax

Fax messages can be sent to persons that use fax machines.

12. Fun And Entertainment

You can find films, cartoons, audio and video songs on internet.

13. **Education**

    There many web sites that provides educational facilities. So education can be achieved online.

14. **News Papers**

    Now many newspapers have their websites. We can read news from internet now.

15. **Download Free Software**

    We can download (save in our computer) free software from internet.

16. **Upload Information**

    We can upload information (send from our computer) on internet. So that this information will be available for internet users.

17. **Hotel Reservation**

    You can get reserved a room for you in a hotel. Several hotels are online now.

18. **Online Shopping**

    You can do all types of shopping on internet.

19. **Download Games**

    You can download computer games from internet.

20. **Traveling Guides**

    You can find information about any country of the world on internet. You can find maps of any country and big cities.

DISADVANTAGES OF INTERNET

1. **Hacking**

   Hackers access the important information and programs and may destroy it. Hackers try to get password of internet users and then access important information.

2. **Computer Virus**

   Computer virus is a program developed for some destructive purpose. Computer virus can destroy your data or software. Virus enters into your computer by internet, floppy disc, CD or USB flash memory drive. Antivirus software like Norton Antivirus and Mcafee Antivirus are used to find and remove virus.

3. Wastage of Time

There are so many interesting facilities on internet. So people use internet for several hours. In this way valuable time is wasted.

4. Educational Loss of Students

Students spend much time in internet café. So they waste their time and do not attend their studies properly.

5. Online Robbery

Important documents are stolen on internet. Passwords of credit cards are stolen on internet. This can do financial loss.

6. Immoral Web Sites

There are many immoral sites on internet. This is destroying high values of the societies that don't allow such sexual material or illegal sexual relations.

5.4 Define Web Server, Web Browser, WWW, ISP

Q. Write notes on the following:
WWW, ISP, WEB PAGE, WEB SITE, WEB SERVER, WEB BROWSER

WWW

WWW stands for World Wide Web. It is also called web. It is the collection of all connected web documents stored on different web servers. These documents contain information in the form of text, pictures, audio and video clips. WWW has many advantages:

- finding a job
- searching information
- advertisement for business
- weather forecast
- entertainment
- education

Difference between Internet and World wide web:

The main difference between internet and World Wide web is that World Wide Web is only a service provided by internet. It provides access to web documents. While internet provides many other services also like FTP, TELNET and chatting etc.

ISP (Internet Service Provider) OR IAP (Internet Access Provider

ISP stands for internet service provider. It is a company that provides internet connections to users. For example WOL net, PAK net, CYBER net etc. are ISPs. To connect to internet, users have to get internet connection from an ISP. These days, internet scratch cards are also available. ISP will provide you a user name, password. It will also provide a telephone number to connect to internet.

There are many ISPs these days in every big city of the country. A good ISP has the following features:

- Low rate
- Fast browsing
- Fast downloading and uploading
- Good customer support

WEB PAGE

A document created by HTML and found on web is a web page. A web page contains information in the form of text, pictures, audio and video clips. These web pages are stored on special computers called WEB SERVERS.

Web Site

A collection of related and interlinked web pages is called a web site. A web site may have many pages. Each web page will provide different information. For example, a web site for a College can have a Home page, Faculty page, Courses page, Games page and contact page. Home page is the main page of any web site. We can see all other pages by links provided in home page. Each web site has a unique address. For example web address of Baha-ud-din Zakaria University is www.bzu.edu.pk.

Web Server

Web documents are stored on special and powerful computers called WEB SERVERS. Web servers are permanently connected to internet. When we type address of a web site in a browser (internet explorer), then web server fulfills this request. They provide requested information in the form of web page.

Web Browser

A browser is software that is used to view web pages on internet. Many web browsers are available. But Mozilla Firefox, Google Chrome and Internet explorer are the most popular. We type address of any web site in address bar of browser and press ENTER key. Then first page called HOME PAGE of web site is displayed in browser window.

Explain Advantages of Networks

ADVANTAGES OF COMPUTER NETWORKS

Following are some important advantages of computer networks:

1. Data and Information Sharing

Different employees of an organization can share common information with the help of computer network.

2. Software Sharing

Different software can be shared with the help of computer networks.

3. Hardware Sharing

Different hardware can be shared with the help of computer networks. For example, if there are five computer users in an office, we can save cost by using only one printer with the help of computer networking. In a computer network, only one computer will manage all printing needs of the computer users in a small office. In addition, we can share other hard ware devices like hard disks, CD-ROM Drives / Writers, modems, routers and scanners etc.

4. Money Saving

We can save a lot of money by using computer networking, because of sharing the same software and hardware in a network.

5. Internet Sharing

We can buy only one DSL internet connection and share it with in whole organization with the help of computer networking.

6. Easy Communication within Organization

We can send and receive messages and files through network. In this way, a file can be moved to one place to another within an organization without the need of a physical worker to take and carry the files to a destination. With the help of a command in a computer we can transfer file within seconds from one room to another.

7. Easy Communication outside Organization

We can send and receive emails and share files with other people outside organization using internet.

Types of Computer Networks

Explain different types of computer networks : (LAN, WAN, MAN)

Main types of computer networks are:

1. LAN - Local-Area Network
2. WAN - Wide-Area Network
3. MAN - Metropolitan-Area Network

(1) LAN (Local Area Network)

LAN stands for Local Area Network. It covers a small area. Most LANs are used to connect computers in a single building or group of near buildings. Hundreds or thousands of computers may be connected through LAN. LANs are used in office buildings, college or university campus etc. Local Area Networks can transfer data at a very high speed. Data transmission speeds of LAN are 1 to 100 megabits per second.

Examples:

Following are two examples of LAN:

- LAN is used in a computer lab to connect computers. The students can share software, files and data in the lab.
- In Internet cafe, many computers can be connected through LAN. These computers can share single connection of Internet.
- Local Area Network can be used in an office to share common data and a network printer and any other software or hardware.
- A local area network in a digital library can provide access to centralized collection of digital books for many readers using different computers in library building.

(2) WAN (Wide Area Network)

WAN stands for wide area network. It covers a large area. WAN connects computers in different cities, countries and continents. So, Wide Area Networks are used to transfer data over very long distances across cities, countries or even in whole world. WANs are used to connect LANs and other types of networks together, so that users and computers in one location can communicate with users and computers in other locations.

Computers in WAN are often connected through leased lines telephone lines. They can also be connected through satellites. Transmission rate of WAN is 56 kbps to 45 Mbps. WAN is expensive than LAN. WAN is not as fast as LAN. There is a possibility of error in data transmission due to very long distance they cover. The largest WAN is the Internet. With the help of internet, we can send our data in any part of the world.

Examples of WAN

In airline ticketing system, many offices of an airline company can be joined together using WAN. A person can get a ticket from any office in the country.

A bank with many branches in different cities can connect its branches through WAN. The customer can use his account from any branch.

(3)MAN (Metropolitan-Area Network)

A metropolitan area network (MAN) is a network that covers an area of the size of a city. So, a MAN is larger than a local area network but it is smaller than a WAN. A MAN is optimized for a larger geographical area than a LAN, ranging from several blocks of buildings to entire cities. MANs can use communications channels of moderate-to-high data transfer rates. It may use fiber Optic cable for fast speeds.

A MAN typically includes one or more LANs but cover a small area than WAN. A MAN often acts as a high-speed network.

Example:

- Mobile phones systems often use MAN.
- Many local ISPs manage MAN with the help of cable modems within a city.
- Local cable TV networks also use MAN technologies.

Differences between LAN and WAN

The differences between LAN and WAN is as follows:

LAN (Local Area Network)

1. LAN is used to connect computers at one place, in one room or a building.

2. LAN covers small and limited area.
3. Data transfer speed is very fast in LAN because of small distance.
4. Local Area network speed is normally form 1 to 100 Mbps.
5. LAN is less costly.
6. LAN is usually connected through wires.
7. Normally, the connection in a LAN is permanent using wires.
8. LAN is used for sharing data, information, files and hardware like printers, hard disk, modem etc.
9. LAN has less possibility of data transmission error.
10. LAN is used to transfer data over small distances.
11. LAN is easy to install and configure.
12. LAN is easy to troubleshoot.

WAN (Wide Area Network)

1. WAN is used to connect computers anywhere in the world.
2. WAN can cover larger area. It can cover cities, countries and even continents.
3. Data transfer speed is slower in WAN.
4. Transmission speeds are normally 56 kbps to 45 Mbps.
5. The hardware needed for a WAN is more expensive.
6. WAN is usually connected through telephone lines, fiber optic cable or through wireless media.
7. The connection in WAN may not be permanent.

8. WAN is used to share only data and information like Email and file transfer

9. WAN has more possibility of data transmission error because of long distance.

10. WAN is used to transfer data over long distances.

11. WAN is difficult to install and configure due to connecting computers at multiple and distant sites.

12. WANs are difficult to troubleshoot

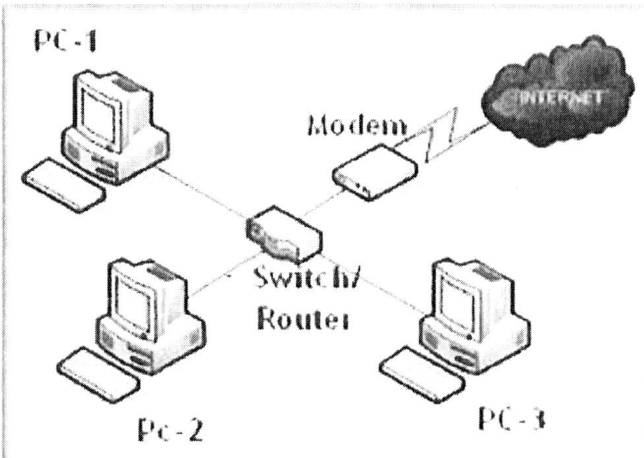

A Local Area Network Diagram (Star Topology)

6

Introduction to Algorithms

6.1 What is an algorithm?

An algorithm is a precise, step-by-step set of instructions for solving a task. An algorithm does not solve a task; it gives you a series of steps that, if executed correctly, will result in a solution to a task. You use algorithms every day but you often do not explicitly think about the individual steps of the algorithm. For example, starting your car, putting on your clothes, logging into your computer, or following a recipe for cooking a food dish, are all accomplished using an algorithm, a step-by-step series of actions.

For an algorithm to be valid, each step (or instruction) must be:

- unambiguous – the instruction can only be interpreted in one unique way
- Executable – the person or device executing the instruction must know how to accomplish the instruction without any extra information.
- Ordered – the steps of an algorithm must be ordered in a proper sequence to correctly accomplish the task.

An example algorithm is shown in the seven steps below. This algorithm explains how to make "frozen lemon ice-box pie," (which is this author's favorite dessert).

Step 1: Pour 1 can of chilled pet milk into a mixing bowl.

Step 2: Beat the pet milk until peaks form.

Step 3: "Fold in" 1 cup of sugar and 1/2 cup of lemon juice.

Step 4: If you want a more lemony taste, add 1 tsp of grated lemon peal.

Step 5: Spread a graham cracker crust on the bottom of a 13" by 9" pan.

Step 6: Pour the pet milk mix into the pan.

Step 7: Place in freezer until frozen.

Before leaving this example, ask yourself if the steps to this algorithm meet the criteria listed above. That is, is each step unambiguous, executable, and in the correct order?

This reading explains the concept of algorithms, some important properties of algorithms, and how algorithms are created, executed, and validated.

6.2 What is Algorithmic Thinking?

Algorithmic thinking is the ability to *understand, execute, evaluate,* and *create* algorithms. Let's discuss each of these ideas separately.

To be an *algorithmic thinker* you need the ability to *understand* and *execute* algorithms. Some people find it easy to follow a series of precise instructions while other people find it very challenging. Some people seem to lack the patience and diligence required to follow a step-by-step plan. However, it is a valuable skill that all people should master. Algorithmic thinking requires patience because each instruction must be executed in its correct sequence without skipping ahead or "glossing over" some of the instructions. In addition, algorithmic thinking requires diligence and perseverance. It is often tedious to follow the steps of a complex algorithm and people sometimes fail to complete an algorithm because they simply "give up."

Algorithmic thinking also requires the ability to *evaluate* algorithms. This involves determining if an algorithm really does solve a given task. This can be very challenging. For example, a "preflight check list" is an algorithm for preparing an aircraft for take off. Suppose you were given the job of determining if a new "preflight check list" for the F35 (Joint Strike Fighter) is *correct* (checks all systems on the aircraft properly) and *complete* (does not leave out any important checks). Hopefully you would agree that this is an important job – pilot's lives are dependent on getting it right – and that getting the check list correct and complete will not be easy. (As a side note, one way to create the preflight check list is to determine the fault of each new aircraft crash and add a new check to the list to prevent future crashes. But the cost in lives and money is too great. We need to get the algorithm correct and complete before the first plane takes to flight to prevent a single aircraft loss!)

And finally, *Algorithmic thinking* includes the ability to *create* new algorithms. This is probably the most challenging aspect of algorithmic thinking. Given a task, can you create a series of precise, step-by-step instructions that always solves the task correctly? Obviously the complexity of the task has a big impact on the complexity of an algorithmthat will accomplish the task.Simple tasks can typically be accomplished with simple algorithms, while complex tasks typically require more complex algorithms.

A critical aspect of algorithm creation is the "target executer" of an algorithm. For example, the "target executer" of a preflight check list is a pilot. The average person on the street could not execute the preflight check list correctly because they would not understand the instructions. The three, previously stated, characteristics of an algorithm instruction (i.e., an instruction must be unambiguous, executable, and ordered) must be consistent with the knowledge and expertise of the "target executer." When you create an algorithm, make sure that each instruction can be unambiguously interpreted and executed by the "target executer."

We live in the "information age," where many of the tasks people need (or want) to do can be accomplished by computers. However, computers currently have no real understanding or cognition – they can only perform tasks that people have developed algorithms to solve. Therefore, to create algorithms that computers can execute, you must understand what a computer is capable of executing and be able to write a series of unambiguous instructions that a computer can execute successfully. For the remainder of this document we will restrict our discussion to the development of algorithms that can be executed on computers.

6.3 How are algorithms communicated?

Each step (instruction) of an algorithm must be precisely stated. It is very difficult to explain algorithms precisely using only the English language. For example, please re-read the example algorithm for making "frozen lemon ice-box pie" and then answer the following questions:

- Does pet milk come in different size containers? How much milk is "1 can"?
- Does it matter what types of beaters are used to beat the pet milk?
- Is "tsp" a teaspoon or a table spoon?

If you tried to implement the recipe to make frozen lemon ice-box pie you might very well discover other ambiguities in the instructions. To eliminate these "communication problems," we need a precise language for specifying algorithms, especially since our "target executioner" is a dumb computer. A precise language for stating the instructions of an algorithm that can be executed by a computer is called a "programming language."

Many programming languages have been developed over the years and each language has its own special features and benefits. You have probably heard of some of these languages, such as C, C++, Pascal, BASIC, Java, Perl, Python, and Ada. It requires a significant amount of time to learn a new programming language and it is not a goal of CS110 to teach you how to program computers. We want cadets to become better problem solvers by becoming algorithmic thinkers. One of the common ways to express algorithms without using a programming language is called flowcharting. Flowcharts provide a visual description of a step-by-step process. The major drawback to using flowcharts is that they are tedious to draw and hard to modify if they are hand drawn on paper. A computer program called RAPTOR was developed by Dr. Carlisle here at USAFA which allows a person to create an algorithm in flowchart form and then actually execute the flowchart to test its validity. Pretty cool! We will discuss the details of how to use RAPTOR in future lessons.

6.4 Why are Algorithms Important?

Algorithms are important for many reasons:

- An algorithm documents the "how to" for accomplishing a particular task.
- If an algorithm is written well, it can be used to accomplish not only a single task but a whole group of related tasks.
- The existence of an algorithm means that the task can potentially be automated (i.e., performed by a computer).
- The automation of redundant, tedious, or dangerous tasks frees people from having to perform these boring, time-consuming, or potentially lethal tasks.

- The automation of some tasks makes new things possible (e.g., accessing web pages from all over the entire world in the blink of an eye).

Consider telephones for example. When telephones were invented, the problem of how to connect one phone caller to another caller arose. For many years this problem was solved manually by phone operators who pulled wires from a console and plugged them into the correct connecting wire. It has been estimated that if this manual method was still used today to handle the current daily phone calls made around the world, every person on the planet would have to be a phone operator! Thankfully, given the invention of fast computers and algorithms to instruct those computers, almost all phone calls made today are automatically connected without human intervention. What would your life be like without a phone? Can you imagine it? Without algorithms, that is the way life would be!

We study algorithms in CS110 because algorithmic thinking is transferable. If you can think and reason precisely and solve algorithmic problems in one domain (e.g. computer programming), then your ability to analyze and solve problems in other areas will improve.

6.5 What are the important properties of algorithms?

The following is a list of some of the important properties of algorithms. This list is by no means comprehensive or complete.

Property 1: For any given, non-trivial task (or set of related tasks), there are many possible algorithms for accomplishing the task.

This greatly confuses many students. "You mean there is more than one correct answer?" The answer is YES! Remember, an algorithm is not the solution to a problem; it is a step-by-step set of instructions for finding a solution. Is there only one way to get from Mitchell Hall to Arnold Hall?

Property 2: An algorithm does not encode the underlying theory behind the instruction steps.

An algorithm tells you how to accomplish a task. If the algorithm is correct, and you follow the instructions exactly, you will accomplish the task. But you may not understand why you did some of the steps. If a computer is executing an algorithm, this lack of understanding is not a problem. If a person is trying to understand an algorithm so that it can be updated or enhanced, this lack of understanding can make changes almost impossible. Complex algorithms often have associated documentation that provides detailed explanations of how they work.

Property 3: Some algorithms are more efficient than other algorithms.

The execution of an algorithm requires some amount of time. If an algorithm is used often, its efficiency becomes an issue. It is common to create multiple algorithms to accomplish a particular task and then select the faster algorithm to include in a final product. One of the challenges of software development is deciding how much time and effort you should expend on the search and development of more efficient algorithms.

Property 4: Computer programs that are used over many years typically must be modified over time to adapt to changes in task requirements.

Computer programs are not typically static objects. They require "maintenance" to keep them current with changes in task requirements. For example, a computer program that calculates income taxes must change every year as the income tax laws change. Some studies have shown that up to 75% of software development costs are consumed by the maintenance of existing software.

In conclusion, when we develop new algorithms, we attempt to create one of many possible sequences of instructions that will solve our task at hand. Ideally we would like the algorithm to execute quickly and be well "commented" so that it can easily be maintained over time.

6.6 An Example – How to create an algorithm

This section will walk you through the process of creating an algorithm for a simple problem. Hopefully you will use the principles discussed here when it comes time for you to develop your own algorithms for different tasks.

Example 1.Exchanging values of two variables

Given two variables X and Y. We have to exchange these variables. TEMP is used for exchanging the variables.

Algorithm

1. INPUT X,Y
2. TEMP ← X

   X ← Y

   Y ← TEMP
3. Write "Exchanged values are", X,Y
4. End .

Example 2. Biggest of three numbers

Given the three numbers X, Y, Z. We have to find the biggest of these

1. INPUT X,Y,Z
2. IF (X>Y) THEN

   Begin

   IF(X>Z) THEN

      Write "Big number is", X

   ELSE

   Write "Big number is", Z

End

ELSE

Begin

IF (Y>Z) then

Write "Big number is ", Y

ELSE

Write big number is ", Z

End

3. END

Example 3.Factorial of a Given Number

Given N number, we have to find the factorial of this number. F denotes the fact of number. Variable I is used to loop counter.

1. Read N
2. F←1
3. I←1
4. WHILE(I<=N)

Begin

F←F*I

I←I+1

End

5. Write "Factorial of a given number is", F
6. End

Example 4. Sum and average of N numbers in an array

Given an array A of N elements. This algorithm finds the sum and average of all the numbers. I denotes array index.

1. SUM!0
2. Repeat for I=1,2,.......N

   SUM!SUM+A [I]
3. AVG!SUM/N
4. Write SUM,AVG
5. END.

Example 5. Matrix multiplication

Given two matrices A and B of orders mxn and pxq respectively. This algorithm multiplies the two matrices (if possible) and stores the result in matrix C (of order (mxq). I, J, K denote array indices.

1. IF n!=p THEN

   Begin

   Write "Matrix multiplication not possible"

   goto step 3

   End
2. Repeat for I=1,2,........,m

   Begin

   Repeat for J=1,2,.......q

   Begin

   C[I<J]!0

   Repeat for K=1,2,.........n

   C[I,J]!C[I,J] + (A[I,K] x B[K,J])

   End

   End
3. End

Example 6: Roots of a quadratic equation (Ax^2 +Bx + C = 0)

```
1. Input A,B,C
2. If A=0 then
   Begin
       If b=0 then
           Begin
               Write "Equation is degenerate"
   goto step 5
           End
       Else
       Begin
           Write "Linear equation has single root"
           x1=-C/B
           Write "Root=", x1
           goto step 5
       End
   End
3. D = B x B – 4.0 X A x C
4. If D>0 then
   Begin
       Write "Real and distinct roots"
       x1=(-B+"D)/(2.0 x A)
       x2=(-B-"D)/(2.0 x A)
       Write "First root=", x1
```

```
Write "Second root=", x2
End
Else
Begin
If (D=0) then
    Write "Real and equal roots"
    Z1=-B/(2.0xA)
    x2=x1
    Write "First root", x1
    Write "Second root", x2
End
Else
Begin
    Write "Imaginary roots"
    x1=-B/(2.0 x A)
    x2=x1
    y1="D/(2.0 x A)
    y2=-y1
    Write "First root"
    Write Real Part", x1, "Img.part", y1
    Write "Second root"
    Write "Real Part", x2, "Img.part", y2
End
End
5. End
```

7

Introduction to Flowcharts

7.1 Introduction of Flowcharts and Flowchart Symbols

What is flowchart?

A flowchart is a graphical representation of an algorithm. These flowcharts play a vital role in the programming of a problem and are quite helpful in understanding the logic of complicated and lengthy problems. Once the flowchart is drawn, it becomes easy to write the program in any high level language. Often we see how flowcharts are helpful in explaining the program to others. Hence, it is correct to say that a flowchart is a must for the better documentation of a complex program.

Flowcharts are usually drawn using some standard symbols; however,

Start or end of the program

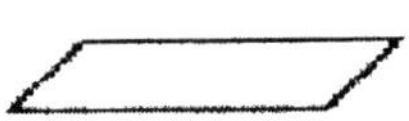

Computational steps or processing function of a program

Input or output operation

Decision making and branching

Connector or joining of two parts of program

Symbol	*Name*	*Purpose*
	**Predefined Process**	A group of statements that together accomplish one task. Used extensively when programs are broken into modules.
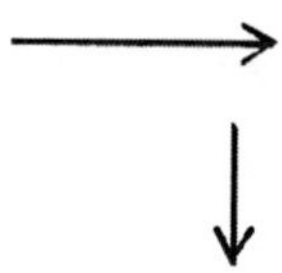	**Flowlines and Arrawheads**	Used to connect symbols and indicate the sequence of operations. The flow is assumed to go from top to bottom and from left to right. Arrowheads are only required when the flow violates the standard direction
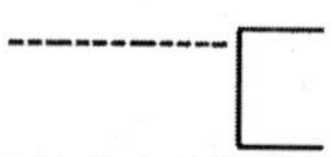	**Annotation**	Can beused to give explanatory comments

The following are some guidelines in flowcharting:

a. In drawing a proper flowchart, all necessary requirements should be listed out in logical order.

b. The flowchart should be clear, neat and easy to follow. There should not be any room for ambiguity in understanding the flowchart.

c. The usual direction of the flow of a procedure or system is from left to right or top to bottom.

d. Only one flow line should come out from a process symbol.

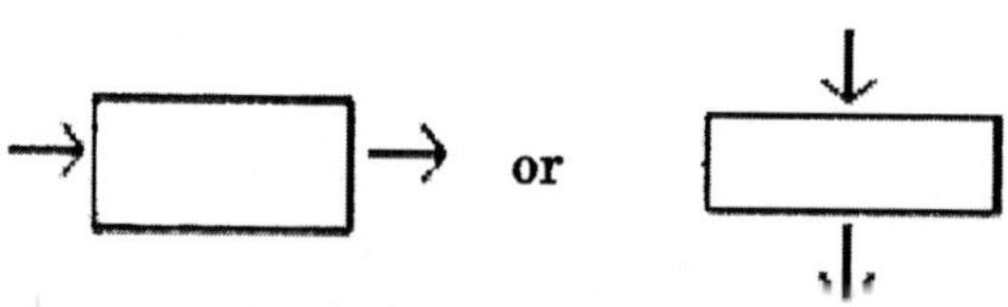

e. Only one flow line should enter a decision symbol, but two or three flow lines, one for each possible answer, should leave the decision symbol.

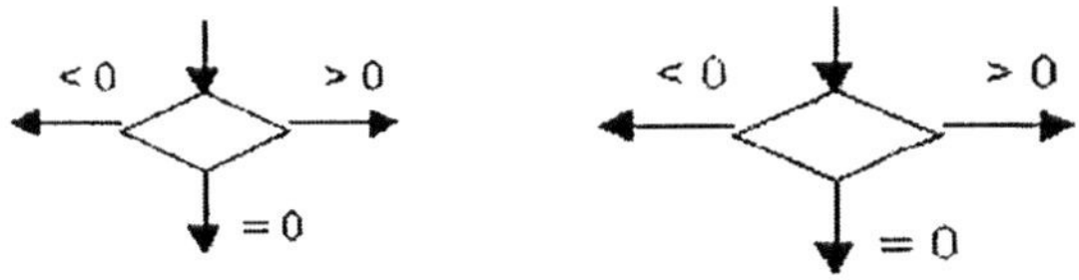

f. Only one flow line is used in conjunction with terminal symbol.

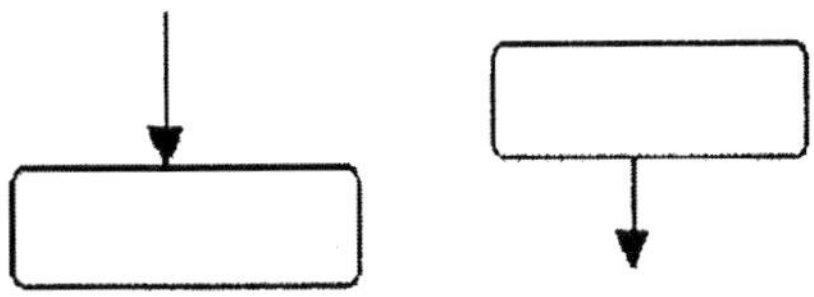

h. If the flowchart becomes complex, it is better to use connector symbols to reduce the number of flow lines. Avoid the intersection of flow lines if you want to make it more effective and better way of communication.

i. Ensure that the flowchart has a logical *start* and *finish*.

j. It is useful to test the validity of the flowchart by passing through it with a simple test data.

7.2 Example of a flowchart:

Problem 1: Write an algorithm and draw the flowchart for finding the average of two numbers

<u>Algorithm:</u>

Input: two numbers x and y

Output: the average of x and y

Steps:

1. input x
2. input y
3. sum = x + y
4. average = sum /2
5. output average

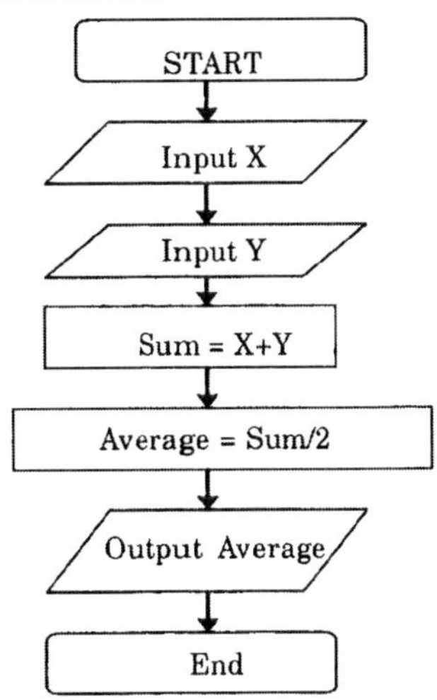

Problem 2. Swapping two numbers

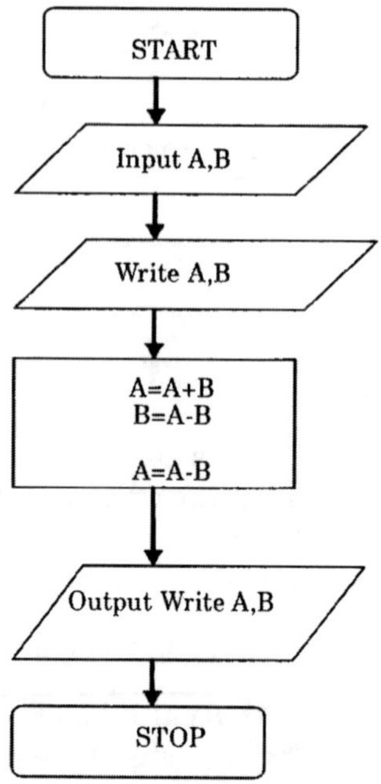

Problem. 3 Finding the biggest of three numbers

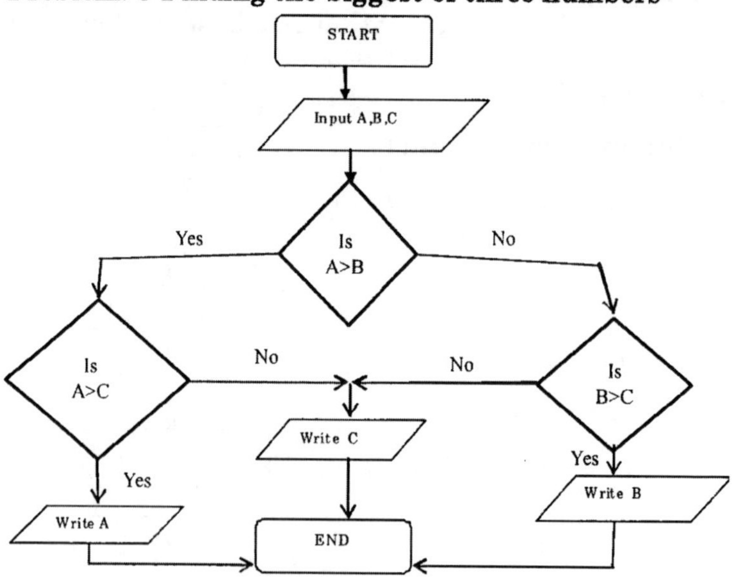

7. **Networking**
   Operating system provides access to shared resources by networking system.

8. **Command Interpreter system**
   Operating system provides command interpreter for reading and executing user commands.

8.2 Functions of operating system

Functions of Operating System

Following are the main functions performed by Operating System:

1. **Process Management**
   CPU can perform one task at one time. If there are many tasks, operating system decides which task should get the CPU first. Operating system also maintains a queue of jobs for processing one by one.

2. **Main Memory Management**
   Operating system manages memory (RAM)for many running programs. It allocates memory area to different programs. It de-allocates the memory area when a program is terminated. It also manages efficient use of RAM during processing.

3. **Secondary Storage Management**
   Operating system manages secondary storage. It manages the stored files and folders on disk in a proper way.

   You can create and save files and folders, edit files, copy files, move files from one location to another within one computer or from computer to computer, and delete files and folders etc, with the help of operating system.

4. **I/O System management**
   It manages Input/output operations. It controls I/O devices like mouse, keyboard, monitor and printer etc.

5. **File Management**
   It manages files, for example:

- creation of files
- deletion of files
- copying of files.
- editing files
- moving of files etc.

6. **Protection System**
   There are many processes of different users in memory at a time. So operating system provides protection so that no process can interfere with another process activity. Operating system makes sure that each and every process performs within its own boundaries.

7. **Networking**
   Operating system provides access to shared resources by networking system. Users can share files and hardware resources like printer.

8. **Command Interpreter system**
   Operating system provides command interpreter for reading and executing user commands. For example, Microsoft Windows XP provides Command Prompt to enter and execute commands.

9. **Booting**
   Operating system starts the computer. It checks the computer and makes it ready to work.

10. **Loading and Execution**
    Operating system provides the facility to load programs in memory easily and then execute it.

11. **Data Security**
    Operating system protects the data stored on the computer from illegal use, modification or deletion.

12 Device Controlling

Operating system controls all devices attached to computer with the help of device drivers. Device driver is a software that permits a computer system to communicate with a device. e.g., device driver software for a modem comes with it on CD. We have to install device driver before using a device.

13. Printing Controlling

Operating System also controls printing function. If a user issues two or more print commands at a time, it manages print queue for printing each document one by one in a proper sequence.

14. Providing Interface

Operating system provides User interface to interact with the computer. User Interface may be Graphical user interface (GUI) or Command line interface. For example, Microsoft Windows XP provides an easy to use graphical user interface called GUI. Whereas DOS provides a Command Line Interface called CLI.

Problem 4. Print the multiplication table of an integer

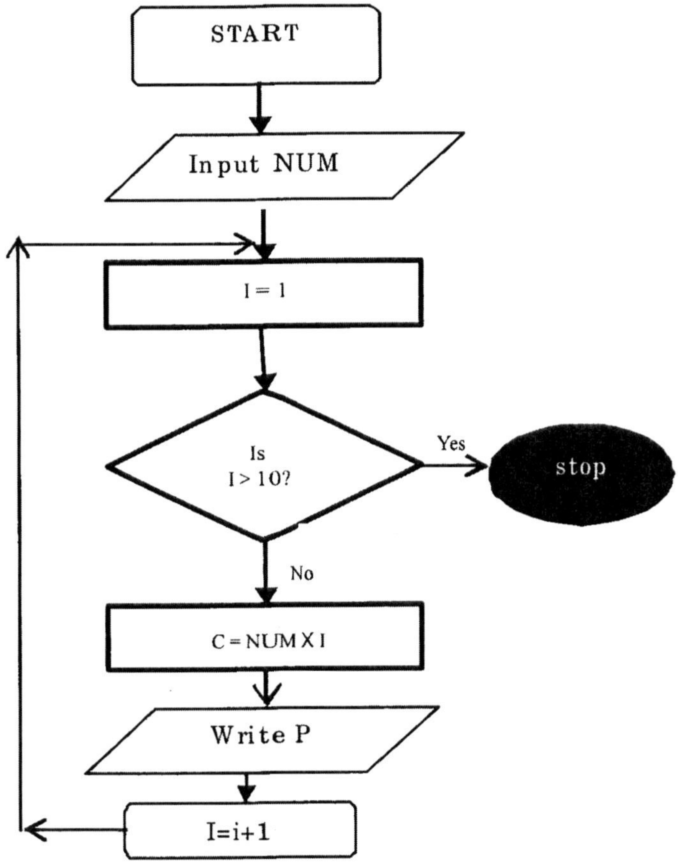

8

Operating System Concept

8.1 Components of Operating System

Q. What is an Operating System? Explain Components of an Operating system.

Operating System

An operating system is a set of programs that manages all computer components and operations. Some popular

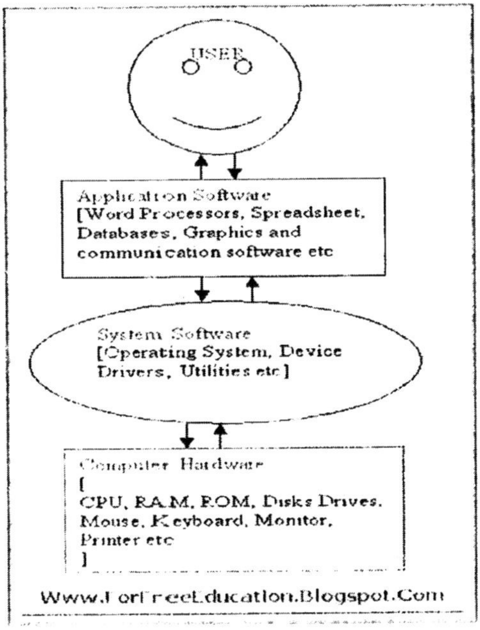

operating systems are DOS, windows, Unix, Linux, and OS/2.

Without Operating System, a computer cannot do anything. Users interact with the computer through operating system. Operating system acts as an interface between a user and computer hardware.

An Operating system has many components to manage all resources of a computer system as following:

1. **Process Management**
   CPU can perform one task at one time. If there are many tasks, operating system decides which task should get the CPU first.

2. **Main Memory Management**
   Operating system manages memory (RAM)for many running programs. It allocates memory area to different programs. It deallocates the memory area when a program is terminated.

3. **Secondary Storage Management**
   Operating system manages secondary storage. It manages the stored files and folders on disk in a proper way.

4. **I/O System management**
   It manages Input/output operations. It controls I/O devices like mouse, keyboard, monitor and printer etc.

5. **File Management**
   It manages files for example creation and deletion of files.

6. **Protection System**
   There are many processes of different users in memory at a time. So operating system provides protection so that no process can interfere with another process activity.

7. **Networking**
   Operating system provides access to shared resources by networking system.

8. **Command Interpreter system**
   Operating system provides command interpreter for reading and executing user commands.

8.2 Functions of operating system

Functions of Operating System

Following are the main functions performed by Operating System:

1. **Process Management**
   CPU can perform one task at one time. If there are many tasks, operating system decides which task should get the CPU first. Operating system also maintains a queue of jobs for processing one by one.

2. **Main Memory Management**
   Operating system manages memory (RAM)for many running programs. It allocates memory area to different programs. It de-allocates the memory area when a program is terminated. It also manages efficient use of RAM during processing.

3. **Secondary Storage Management**
   Operating system manages secondary storage. It manages the stored files and folders on disk in a proper way.

   You can create and save files and folders, edit files, copy files, move files from one location to another within one computer or from computer to computer, and delete files and folders etc, with the help of operating system.

4. **I/O System management**
   It manages Input/output operations. It controls I/O devices like mouse, keyboard, monitor and printer etc.

5. **File Management**
   It manages files, for example:

- creation of files
- deletion of files
- copying of files.
- editing files
- moving of files etc.

6. **Protection System**
   There are many processes of different users in memory at a time. So operating system provides protection so that no process can interfere with another process activity. Operating system makes sure that each and every process performs within its own boundaries.

7. **Networking**
   Operating system provides access to shared resources by networking system. Users can share files and hardware resources like printer.

8. **Command Interpreter system**
   Operating system provides command interpreter for reading and executing user commands. For example, Microsoft Windows XP provides Command Prompt to enter and execute commands.

9. **Booting**
   Operating system starts the computer. It checks the computer and makes it ready to work.

10. **Loading and Execution**
    Operating system provides the facility to load programs in memory easily and then execute it.

11. **Data Security**
    Operating system protects the data stored on the computer from illegal use, modification or deletion.

12 Device Controlling

Operating system controls all devices attached to computer with the help of device drivers. Device driver is a software that permits a computer system to communicate with a device. e.g., device driver software for a modem comes with it on CD. We have to install device driver before using a device.

13. Printing Controlling

Operating System also controls printing function. If a user issues two or more print commands at a time, it manages print queue for printing each document one by one in a proper sequence.

14. Providing Interface

Operating system provides User interface to interact with the computer. User Interface may be Graphical user interface (GUI) or Command line interface. For example, Microsoft Windows XP provides an easy to use graphical user interface called GUI. Whereas DOS provides a Command Line Interface called CLI.